PREACH THE WORD

Towards effective grassroots preacher training in sub-Saharan Africa.

Myles MacBean

WIPF & STOCK · Eugene, Oregon

Wipf and Stock Publishers
199 W 8th Ave, Suite 3
Eugene, OR 97401

Preach the Word
Towards Effective Grassroots Preacher Training in Sub-Saharan Africa
By MacBean, Myles
Copyright©2017 Apostolos
ISBN 13: 978-1-5326-6956-9
Publication date 9/23/2018
Previously published by Apostolos, 2017

There remains a well-documented shortage of theologically sound, Bible-centric preaching in sub-Saharan Africa, where most sermons are preached by church leaders who are either untrained or undertrained.

Following a practical theology praxis, this study develops a conceptual framework for the evaluation of existing "alternative" approaches to grassroots preacher training in Africa based on a review of the theology of preaching and of preacher training, and on "imported" knowledge from theological education and business-oriented fields. Three broad principles for effective preacher training are proposed: contextualisation, scalability, and sustainability.

This framework is applied to a case study of preacher training in the challenging context of the Zambezi Evangelical Church (ZEC) of Malawi, with the aim of discovering what ZEC's experience reveals about the viability of contextual, scalable and sustainable grassroots preacher training in sub-Saharan Africa.

Qualitative and quantitative information on ZEC and its needs was gathered by interviewing leaders in the organisation, and through a broader survey of elders and pastors. The character of selected church leader training programs in sub-Saharan Africa was also evaluated through interview and document analysis.

The fieldwork confirmed ZEC as serving in a very challenging spiritual context, but with a leadership who recognised the priority of transforming grassroots preaching. Training programs active in sub-Saharan Africa and Malawi also demonstrated many of the features required if contextual, scalable, and sustainable grassroots preacher training is to be feasible.

However, it was concluded that for such training to be genuinely viable in this context, ZEC needs to ensure that its organisational culture and values are transformed. Equally, training programs need to become even more intentional in their aspirations to be contextual, scalable, and sustainable. This results in specific recommendations for ZEC and preacher training programs in Malawi. The analytical framework and broad conclusions are also found to warrant wider consideration in sub-Saharan Africa.

Finally, a postscript to the original 2015 study provides an overview of the design of a grassroots preacher training course ("Preach the Word") which aims to implement the recommendations of this study.

Acknowledgements

This study would not have been possible without the enthusiastic support of Zambesi Mission and Zambezi Evangelical Church. I thank particularly Mike Beresford, Mission Director of ZM, Simon Chikwana, Field Director of ZM, and Luckwell Mtima, General Secretary of ZEC.

Special thanks must also go to the many research partners involved in the study who must remain anonymous: to the wide range of executives, pastors, and elders of ZEC who so openly and enthusiastically engaged with me on our mutual interest in preaching; and to the leaders of training programs who so generously gave of their time and wisdom.

Thanks is also due to Edson Kamukira, who so conscientiously accompanied me on my travels, interpreted during the interviews, and translated surveys returned in Chichewa.

Thanks also to the staff of Moorlands College, and in particular my supervisor Chris Sinkinson, who so ably introduced me to the principles and values of practical theology.

I also gratefully acknowledge the partnership of Disciple the Nations (Malawi) whose expertise and experience of grassroots training in Malawi has allowed the "Preach the Word" training program to be developed and piloted so effectively.

I am also grateful to Mathew Bartlett and the team at Apostolos Publishing for their support and for their mission-oriented outlook.

Finally, I thank my wife and research assistant, Ruth. Yet again her patience, love, and support—not least in her heroic transcription of over thirty hours of interview recordings—have helped guide me through my academic trials.

Abbreviations

The following key abbreviations have been used throughout this study.

CPM Church Planting and Multiplication.

CSF Critical Success Factor(s)

DTE Diversified Theological Education

E1 Existing Programs (e.g. E1, E2 etc.) – The training programs reviewed in this study that are already working with ZEC members in some way in Malawi.

LSQ Learning Style Questionnaire – the learning style model and methodology developed by Honey and Mumford.

N1 "National Executive 1" etc. – Sequentially numbered anonymous code for interviewed national executives of ZEC.

P1 Potential Programs (e.g. P1, P2 etc.) – The training programs reviewed that are not yet working in Malawi or with ZEC members.

R1 "Regional Executive 1" etc. – Sequentially numbered anonymous code for interviewed regional executives of Zambezi Evangelical Church.

TEE Theological Education by Extension

ZEC Zambezi Evangelical Church

ZM Zambesi Mission

Contents

PROLOGUE 2

ACKNOWLEDGEMENTS 5

ABBREVIATIONS 6

INTRODUCTION 11

CHAPTER 1: MODELLING EFFECTIVENESS 14

PRACTICAL THEOLOGY PRAXIS 14
THEOLOGY 14
   Theology of Preaching 15
   Theology of Preacher Training 17
CONTEXT 18
   Malawi 18
   Zambezi Evangelical Church 19
   Learning in Context 20
   Preaching in Context 21
OTHER SOURCES OF KNOWLEDGE 22
   Diversified Theological Education 22
   Training Needs 24
   Training Principles 25
   Coaching 26
   Franchise Management 27
   Church Planting and Multiplication 28
CONCLUSIONS ON CONCEPTUAL FRAMEWORK 29

CHAPTER 2: EVALUATING EFFECTIVENESS 31

DESIGN 31
ETHICS 31
METHODS 32
   Semi-Structured Interview 32
   Guided Questionnaire 33
   Existing Document Analysis 33
   Self-Guided Survey 33
   Learning Styles 34
PROCESS 34
   Interview and Guided Questionnaire of Users 34
   Interview and Guided Questionnaire of Providers 35
   Self-Guided Survey 35

CHAPTER 3: ANALYSING ZEC 36

ANALYTICAL TOOLS 36
   Quantitative 36
   Qualitative 36

  Triangulation and Comparison 36
 User Results and Analysis 37
  ZEC Research Partners 37
  ZEC Context 37
  ZEC Churches 38
  ZEC Preachers 38
  ZEC Preaching 39
  ZEC Learning Styles 40
  ZEC Preaching Styles 41
  ZEC Perspectives on Preacher Training 42
 Provider Results and Analysis 44
  Provider Research Partners 44
  ZEC and Africa Context 45
  Importance of Preaching and Preacher Training 45
  Evaluating Training Methods 46
  Program Profiles, Goals and Principles 46
  Program Approach to Preaching 47
  Program and Critical Success Factors 48

CHAPTER 4: DISCUSSING ZEC 49

 ZEC Context 49
 ZEC Preaching 50
  Importance and Nature of Preaching 50
  Problems with Preaching 51
  Opportunities 51
 ZEC Learning Style 52
 ZEC Preaching Style 54
 Training 57
  Problems with "Traditional" Models 57
  Importance of Key Components 57
  Challenge of Leadership Culture 58
  Profile of ZEC Needs and Provider Programs 58
  Goals of ZEC and Training Programs 59
  Principles for Preacher Training 60
  Critical Success Factors 64
  Summary Overview of Training Program 65

CHAPTER 5: DOING BETTER 67

 Conclusions 67
  Context 67
  Preaching 67
  Learning 68
  Preacher Training 69
  Framework, Methods and Tools 72
 Recommendations 73

- Providers 73
- ZEC 74
- Wider Church in Malawi and Sub-Saharan Africa 75
- Further Work 75

CHAPTER 6: PREACH THE WORD 78

- ZEC 78
- ZEC TRAINING 79
  - Discipleship Training 79
  - Leadership Training 79
- PREACH THE WORD 80
  - Program development 80
  - Overview 81
  - Module 1: We Preach the Word 83
  - Preaching Journal 87
  - Module 2: We Preach the Whole Word 88
  - Module 3 88
  - College integration 89
- LOOKING FORWARD 89

APPENDIX A – QUANTITATIVE EVALUATION FRAMEWORK 92

- ZEC LEADERSHIP CULTURE 92
- ZEC CONTEXT PROFILE 93
- TRADITIONAL METHODS 94
- ALTERNATIVE METHODS 94
- PREACHER TRAINING 95
  - Training Profile 95
  - Goals 96
  - Principles 96
- CRITICAL SUCCESS FACTORS 97
- PREACHING 97
- LEARNING 99

APPENDIX B – SELECTED RESULTS 100

- ZEC RESULTS AND ANALYSIS 100
  - Context 100
  - Leadership Culture 100
  - Churches 101
  - Preachers 102
  - Preaching 103
  - Preacher Training 104
- PROVIDER RESULTS AND ANALYSIS 106
  - Qualitative Summary 106
  - Context 109
  - Preacher Training 109

DISCUSSION 113
   Problems with 'traditional" methods 113
   Key componants of "alternative" methods 113
APPENDIX C – EXAMPLE SESSION PLANS **114**
   OVERVIEW OF MODULE 1 114
   OVERVIEW OF MODULE 2 115
   MODULE 1: SESSION 1: INTRODUCTION TO PREACHING AND THE PREACHER 116
      1.1 Introduction 116
      1.2 Preaching as a Craft 116
      1.3 Importance of Preaching 117
      1.4 Nature of Preaching 118
      1.5 Expository Preaching 119
   MODULE 1 – SESSION 5: UNDERSTANDING A BIBLE LETTER 122
      5.1 The Style of the Bible Passage 122
      5.2 Characteristics of a Letter 122
      5.3 Bible Letters 123
      5.4 Sculpting a Sermon with a Bible Letter 123
BIBLIOGRAPHY **125**

Introduction

Theological education matters, for God's good purpose in Africa. To my mind in this day, in this hour, on this continent, there is really no higher calling. (Paul Bowers, 2007)[1]

It was in late 2013 that I made my first visit to sub-Saharan Africa and discovered the evangelical church in a complex set of long-standing, Acts-like, crises; yet I also discovered denominational leaders with exceptional vision and courageous faith seeking new ways forward; and discovered a seminal text sitting on a dusty Malawi bookshelf: Kinsler's *Ministry by the People: Theological Education by Extension*.[2] A life-changing personal journey had started.

Of course, my personal journey was not a new one. Paul was there ahead of me, and he laid out a clear analysis of the situation in Rom 10:14–17. Just as in Paul's day the problems faced by the Church in sub-Saharan Africa are fundamentally spiritual, the necessary spiritual renewal of faith can still only come from the "message" of the "word of Christ," and—especially in oral cultures with few Bibles like rural Africa—that message will still be primarily "heard" by the people through someone "preaching to them." So, the age-old problem remains: "how can anyone preach unless they are sent?" (Romans 10:15) Hence, as Bowers identified a decade ago, there is probably still no higher calling in sub-Saharan Africa today than the equipping and releasing of preachers through theological education.

Neither is it new to consider such theological matters in a cross-cultural context, for it was in the 19th century that the missionary leaders Rufus Anderson and Henry Venn recognised the need for cross-cultural ministry to be grassroots indigenous and hence "self-propagating, self-governing, and self-supporting" if it was to be truly effective.[3] With a mindset much shaped by business, I quickly found myself reframing this famous "three-self formula" as the requirement for theological education programs to be: *contextual, scalable,* and *sustainable.*

As well as bringing a focus on rural preaching, and an awareness of the challenges of effective ministry, my early interactions highlighted four highly coupled problems for the church in Africa; problems of a practical and theological nature.

First, the problem of growth. The 20th century had seen the church in Africa grow 36 fold to 360 million in what is arguably "the largest religious change in human history in such a short period," and which helped shift the focus of Christianity from North to South.[4] This rapid growth is – debatably – considered by some missiologists and theologians to have resulted in an African church "a mile wide and an inch deep," i.e. a church of great size but lacking in spiritual depth.[5]

Second, the problem of leadership. The rapid growth has led to insufficient numbers of trained leaders being available to oversee their congregations, even if their congregations could afford them.[6]

Third, the problem of preaching. Those untrained or undertrained leaders (with an inadequate knowledge of scripture, understanding of its interpretation, or skill in communicating its truths) find themselves preaching up to 90% of the sermons in rural Africa.[7]

Finally, the problem of theological education. Despite a tremendous hunger for training among many of those preachers, "traditional" college based theological education cannot keep up with the demand for trained pastors and preachers in an affordable or culturally appropriate manner.[8]

I was certainly not surprised to discover from Kinsler and others that I was not the only one to have noticed these issues, and indeed that as early as the 1960s it had been understood by many that the development of mature pastors was the "primal" challenge for the church in Africa, and that "alternative" approaches to the training of pastors and preachers were required to meet this challenge.[9] What surprised me was that, over 50 years later, the significant promise of alternative training models such as Theological Education by Extension (TEE) has yet to be fully realised.[10] The fundamental need seemed to remain for "models that will train effective leaders for contexts where the resources are few and the congregations many."[11]

Hence the summer of 2014 was a time of reflection. My former career as a senior business leader had left me with a passion for coaching leaders and an interest in how business principles might be appropriately applied to practical theological issues. In addition, my vocation as a preacher in rural Suffolk had resulted in a passion for faithful expository preaching, while my MA studies in Applied Theology had excited me concerning new homiletic models.[12] My recent involvement in cross-cultural mission had introduced me to radical training models that promised numerical scalability and economic sustainability;[13] and I was on the threshold of new cross-cultural ministry in Malawi partnering with Zambezi Evangelical Church.

It was therefore with a combination of academic theological interest and real personal passion that I concluded that I had a potentially useful contribution to make to this critical ongoing theological and practical problem, and formulated the primary research question for my study:

What does the example of the Zambezi Evangelical Church in Malawi tell us about the viability of training grassroots preachers in sub-Saharan Africa in a way that is contextual, scalable and sustainable?

In this book, I shall give an overview of my research and its findings, before presenting a tentative solution to the practical problem at hand: how can we better equip the preachers of sub-Saharan Africa for their urgent, vital, and God-given ministry?

Chapter 1: Modelling Effectiveness

Practical Theology Praxis

In my study, I tackled the research question by developing a conceptual framework using the principles of practical theology; the first task being to define what it meant to have an "effective" grassroots preacher training program. In theological terms, an explicit theology of preaching and preacher training underpins the conceptual framework. In practical terms the framework sympathetically integrates other "sources of knowledge" with the theology while recognising their "subordinate" status; in that it embraces the idea of a "critical" reflective cycle between the context under study and the biblical theology; and in that it concludes with a "theology of practice" that presents actionable, pragmatic recommendations.[14]

I based my study on the belief that "Truth in the biblical sense has to do with both content and form," and hence a practical focus on "how" (as well as "what") we train rural preachers in sub-Saharan Africa is a legitimate topic for "sensitive theological antennae."[15]

Consequently, my strategy was to embrace a breadth of topics and create value-add through multi-facetted synthesis; bringing to play perspectives from education, psychology, and business management to create a holistic model that could be applied to the practical research question. One might indeed describe it as an "engineering" rather than a "scientific" approach to theology.

Theology

If, as Karl Barth said, "We need to view the study of preaching primarily as a theological concern," the same could surely be said concerning preacher training.[16] The presumed theology of preaching ("what" preachers should be trained) and of preacher training ("how" they should be trained) thus formed a core building block for my study.

Theology of Preaching

Anderson might consider that the "death of the sermon has been greatly exaggerated," but the theological debate over the importance, foundation, function, and form of preaching in the Christian church continues.[17] The majority world is not immune to the objections to preaching that comes with the post-modern challenge to authority and modern lifestyles, and this should perhaps not be surprising in a "last days" context (e.g. 2 Tim 3:1–7).[18] Nevertheless, the analytical framework which underpinned my study held to the following theological propositions:

First, "the priority of preaching" in church life remains paramount.[19] This is seen as a biblical position given, for example: "the authority of the preached word" evident in Deuteronomy; the priority accorded to preaching by Jesus and his disciples (e.g. Acts 6, Rom 10:14–19); and Paul's exhortations to Timothy (e.g. 2 Tim 4:1–2).[20] It is also seen as having a pragmatic importance given the unique effectiveness of preaching in low-tech, cross-cultural communication medium: "Every culture knows what it is to sit and listen to an authoritative being speak."[21] Indeed, for good or ill, "the only means by which many Christians will hear God's Word in the African oral context is through preaching."[22]

Second, that the foundation of preaching is fundamentally expositional, that is it: (a) opens Scripture to understand the original meaning and purpose of the text; (b) looks to communicate that meaning and purpose to today's audience; so that (c) lives might see "gospel transformation" through the work of the Holy Spirit.[23] Again, this principle can be considered biblical and is reflected, for example, in the life of Jesus (e.g. Luke 24:32) and Paul (e.g. Acts 17:2; 2 Tim 4:2).[24]

However, the expositional foundation of preaching does not prescribe any particular function or form of sermon as normative, i.e. limiting it to a function of proclamation, or a form of deductive logic. Instead— being influenced by the "new homiletic"—I understand that inductive and deductive approaches to both the function of a sermon, and the form of a sermon, can be seen to have a biblical basis.[25]

Further, as Anderson emphasises in particular, the use of a variety of homiletic styles between—and even within—sermons can be argued to have considerable value in communicating to people of different cultures, learning styles, and orality in the congregation.[26]

Building on the valuable work of Long and of Anderson (among others), I sought to capture this diversity of homiletic style in the Homiletic Window model which I have described in depth elsewhere (see Fig. 1 below).[27] While it has no rigorous scientific standing or proven instrument validity, I had already usefully applied it to a UK preaching context and I concluded that it would make a valuable contribution to the characterisation of preaching and preacher training in a sub-Saharan setting (see Appendix A, "Preaching").

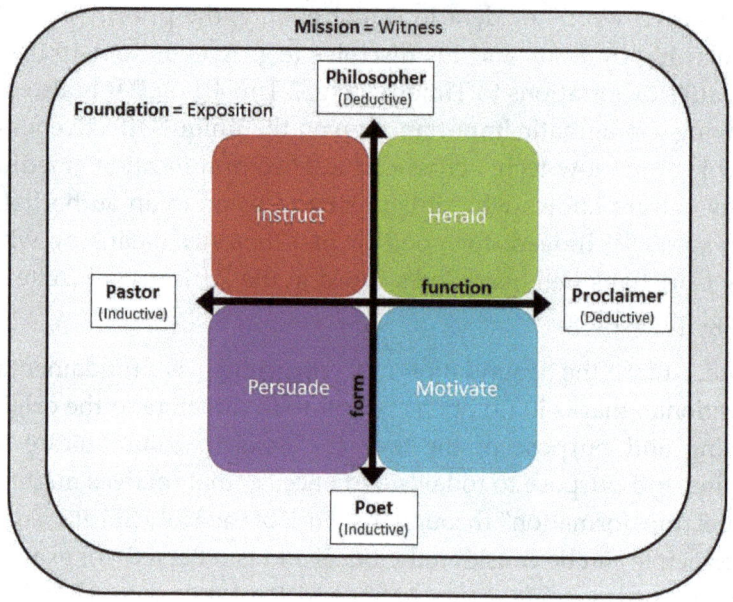

Fig. 1 – The Homiletic Window

In this model, a practitioner's preaching style is categorised on the basis of their perception of the "function" of sermons, and their preferred "form" of sermon. At one extreme the function is considered to be the deductive, declarative proclamation of a message from Scripture, while at the other extreme it is considered the pastoral task of meeting the inductively determined spiritual needs of the listeners. Similarly, at one extreme the preferred form of the sermon is the deductive, cognative, and propositional approach of a philosopher, while at the other extreme it is the inductive and emotive approach of a poet. Following Anderson this results in the four preaching styles that aim to herald, instruct, persuade or motivate the listeners.

Theology of Preacher Training

Having looked at the "what" of preaching, and concluding that the "expository" biblical basis for preaching does not require a narrowly defined normative style, and having recognised with Hovil that it is important to think theologically about "how" we train preachers, I wished to investigate whether there are biblical norms for the style of theological training. [28]

Historically, theological training methods could be considered to include discipleship, catechism, monastery, university, and seminary; with discipleship and seminary arguably the most relevant to my study.[29] Of those two there is a compelling case that discipleship was the exclusive training model in the early church, with Patterson arguing: "It was the only way that Christ and his apostles taught those who were to pastor his church."[30]

Certainly, biblically, we can see discipleship taking place in contexts as diverse as the family (2 Tim 3:10–17) and the local church (Acts 18:26); and we can see it working through the medium of modelling/apprenticeship (Phil 2:19–22), and by coaching through pastoral visits and letters.[31]

Practically speaking, the traditional discipleship model for training can also be seen to have significant strengths in that it involves intimate modelling through a human relationship, hence is implicitly contextual, and will naturally be practical and ministry oriented.[32]

So, while it would be unreasonable for anyone to claim to be able to reproduce the exact New Testament model of Jesus, and while the model has inherent risks, such as limited theological development, nevertheless there appears to be real justification for saying the discipleship model "has the approval (if not the imperative) of scripture;" is a "God-given pattern of formation;" and in the New Testament record has demonstrated itself successful in the low-resource, oral, and relational context that rural Africa finds itself in.[33]

In summary then, I recognise, from the outset, the importance of expository preaching, but I will not argue for any normative function or form for the sermon. I am also—whilst avoiding "primitivism" and not claiming it as an absolute biblical norm—open to the practical value in a sub-Saharan context of alternative training models with a strong discipleship or "on the job" orientation.[34]

Context

My study was undertaken among the local leaders (pastors and elders) and executive (denominational level) leaders of Zambezi Evangelical Church in Malawi. The context in which my research took place must be clearly understood if its conclusions are to be appropriately carried across to other contexts within sub-Saharan Africa and beyond.

Malawi

The Republic of Malawi is a landlocked sub-tropical country located in Southeast Africa with an area roughly half and a population roughly a quarter of the UK. With 20% of that area taken up by Lake Malawi, it is one of the more densely populated countries in sub-Saharan Africa.[35] Formed as the British Central Africa Protectorate in 1891 after a history of British missionary endeavour, Malawi gained its independence in 1964 and is now one of the more peaceful of sub-Saharan nations, with a flourishing multiparty democracy. It uses English as the official language and Chichewa is the national language.[36] A peaceful and welcoming land deserving its title "The Warm Heart of Africa," Malawi is also one of the poorest nations on earth with 83% of its population rural, 51% of the population in poverty, the second lowest Gross National Income per capita in the world, and a Human Development Index ranking of 174 out of 187.[37]

Concerning matters of religion, exact figures are disputed. However, typically over 75% of Malawians are reported as professing Christians, with some 15% described as evangelicals. Though difficult to assess, Muslims may form between 15 and 20% of the population.[38] Data on denominational allegiance is even more unreliable, but the largest Christian groups in Malawi are typically stated as the Roman Catholic Church and the Church of Central Africa, Presbyterian; with the latter the biggest Protestant denomination at a reported 1.3 million membership.[39]

Zambezi Evangelical Church

Zambezi Evangelical Church (ZEC) started in 1892 as Zambezi Industrial Mission (ZIM) which was founded by Joseph Booth with a radical egalitarian vision considered "anti-colonial" by the British administration. It aimed to establish "self-supporting and self-extending" stations, and almost uniquely the mission was self-sustaining for many decades before becoming a Faith Mission (named Zambesi Mission) in the late 1930s.[40]

Starting in Mitsidi near Blantyre, ZIM's influence was initially confined to the Shire Highlands and Southern Ngoniland before the church followed its people to the towns that were developing in Malawi and finally spread across the nation and beyond into (then) Southern Rhodesia and South Africa.

At the time of Malawi independence the indigenous, Malawian-led, ZEC was formed to operate churches, schools and clinics, while the UK-headquartered Zambesi Mission (ZM) continued to act as a Western partner.[41] Today ZEC is one of the largest protestant denominations in Malawi with a membership of approximately 100,000; 220,000 affiliates; 150 churches; and an estimated 5–600 local "prayer houses."[42] It has a conservative evangelical doctrinal position, a Presbyterian form of government, and holds to believers-baptism principles.[43] The church is still headquartered at Mitsidi and remains heavily involved in social service such as education and health. The church is most prominent in the Southern and Central regions of Malawi and, reflecting its origins, its demographic is heavily skewed towards the poorer, rural areas of the country.

Almost all pastors in ZEC hold at least a 3-year undergraduate certificate or diploma in a pastoral or biblical subject. However, the continuing model of a pastor leading a parent church with many prayer houses leaves untrained/semi-trained elders with much of the preaching and pastoring responsibilities.

This contextual analysis reveals ZEC as having many strengths (e.g. an evangelical/biblical tradition) and significant opportunities (e.g. a rural heart and trained indigenous pastors). However, as a large church in a very poor country and with no significant external financial support, it is an especially challenging environment for effective grassroots preacher training.

Learning in Context

In deriving a theology framework for preacher training, I examined alternative discipling/coaching based models potentially appropriate for the context.

However, the limited literature on the topic shows a complex sub-Saharan educational setting. The cultural influence of traditional sub-Saharan training models appears to remain high; a culture where training was based on community driven "apprenticeship" type models and "initiation" rites where "repetition, imitation, internalization and practice" with coach/mentors and "group instruction" was internalised with the aid of "stories and many proverbs."[44] Nevertheless, in modern Malawi these influences are fused with a mainstream education system—originally introduced by missionaries in the late 19th century—that remains distinctly formal and academic.[45]

Another complexity is the divergent views on the influence of culture on an individual's cognitive learning style. Some would argue that "different cultures produce different learning styles," with non-Western peoples exhibiting clear "field-dependent" emphases such as "group cooperation," "relational/holistic" thinking, and symbolism that is "concrete and drawn from everyday life."[46] While these learning preferences would appear consistent with the traditional African training norms, others argue that "within a group, the variations among individuals are as great as their commonalities" and that people need to be treated as individuals.[47] Indeed quantitative studies appear to show that, while culture does influence learning style preference, it is no more powerful than "educational specialisation."[48]

Equally debated is the efficacy of various questionnaires/techniques for testing learning styles in the field.[49] Nevertheless, in 2009 Howles successfully used the "Learning Styles Questionnaire" (LSQ) model of Honey and Mumford with theology students in Uganda.[50] This model recognises a four stage "Learning Cycle" of: (1) having and experience; (2) reviewing that experience; (3) concluding from that experience; and (4) planning the next steps. In this it is very similar to the earlier (1984) model of Kolb, to various problem solving cycles, and indeed to cyclical models for practical theology.[51] While all four stages need to be passed through, and everyone has some ability in each, LSQ recognises that learners will have one (or possibly more) learning style preferences that map on to these stages in the learning cycle: an "Activist" likes to take direct action; a "Reflector" likes to think about things in detail before taking action; a "Theorist" likes to see how things fit into an overall pattern; and a "Pragmatist" likes to see how things work in practice.[52] I therefore decided to use this model to gain a comparable understanding to Howles of learning styles among ZEC preachers, and hence to help determine an appropriate training model for Malawi (see Appendix A, "Learning").

Preaching in Context

Even though I have already argued above for a tentative theology of preaching, it is important to understand the practice of preaching in Malawi. Despite a "dearth of literature on preaching from an African point of view," and an inevitable variety of practices across the continent, the literature does identify certain definite trends.[53]

In terms of hermeneutics, preachers are reported as being "oblivious to the historical context" of a text, showing little in the way of "comprehensive exegesis;"[54] and they are shown to interpret Scripture "literally and uncritically" using a *de facto* "inductive reader-response" approach.[55]

In turn, preparation is described as limited, with overworked preachers relying on a culture of "[i]mpromptu speaking" that results in "superficial sermons" and plagiarism.[56] Favourite subjects and texts are often chosen, with proof texting common, a single verse is usually preferred to a passage, and frequently "no connection whatsoever [is made] between what is preached and the text that was read."[57]

In addition, the message of the sermons is reportedly often rather narrow. It is typically derived from "topical, inductive responses to felt need," with an instructional tone, and a focus on repentance and "personal morality."[58] Indeed in his valuable investigation of preaching in rural Malawi, Chifungo concludes that most sermons are directed at asking Christians to "earn their salvation by living a moral life" or "by repentance of their sins."[59]

If hermeneutics and theological sophistication might be a challenge for the grassroots preacher, contextual homiletics is not: they are "very good orators" in their "oral-cultural" context.[60] The aim is "to reach consensus" rather than win an argument using rich oral techniques where "storytelling is the normative."[61] Emphatic oratory gestures are also combined with substantial audience involvement, repetition, proverbs, idioms, drama, song, and dance.[62]

In summary, my review of the applicable literature has found a context of growing churches, dependent on under-trained or untrained preachers, within an acutely challenging social, cultural, and economic environment, and significant issues with the grassroots preaching culture.

Other Sources of Knowledge

Diversified Theological Education

By the 1960s, in the majority world there was a growing recognition of the limitations of traditional theological training methods.[63] Holland neatly summarised them as not training enough people, not training the right people, and not training people in the right things.[64] I adopted Holland's structure in this study as the "Traditional Methods" model (see Appendix A, "Traditional Methods") and used it to test perception concerning problems with traditional training methods.

This critique resulted in a multitude of alternative models for theological education, with a focus on "pastoral education on a poverty level."[65] The most prominent is Theological Education by Extension (TEE) which in Africa can be traced back to Kenya in 1969 and which some argue should be the norm for majority world theological training.[66]

Classic TEE is a tripartite model combining home study (cognitive learning), small group seminars (group interaction), and ministerial practice (experience).[67] These three components formed a useful framework against which to verify the perceived importance of different elements of alternative training programs (see Appendix A, "Alternative Methods").

The claimed benefits of TEE appear particularly relevant to the context of this study. Quantitatively, TEE is said to help overcome the capacity limitations of traditional college models, reduce the cost compared to those traditional models, and open up training to grassroots "natural leaders."[68] Importantly, some also implement trainer multiplication strategies.[69] Proponents also claim qualitative benefits including a greater emphasis on experience; on "ministry by the people;" on equipping the right people; on ministry formation; on keeping the students involved in their context; and on developing culturally relevant material.[70]

While such "alternatives to the schooling model" of theological education have "attained recognition and accreditation within the mainstream," and given the identified benefits, it is perhaps surprising that 50 years on TEE is not more prevalent in majority world theological education.[71] While it is difficult to objectively evaluate TEE, the literature identifies several systemic issues with the model which might provide part of the answer. These include: a tendency towards control and dependence, over reliance on texts and other written resources, and the relegation of discipling elements of training.[72] Additional contextual challenges identified include: resistance from the existing ordained ministry, resistance to the perceived imposition of alternative models, inadequate contextualisation of material, and dissatisfaction with the low academic level of the program or its doctrinal positions.[73] Notably, it is also emphasised that TEE can be severely weakened if any individual component is "weak, missing, or misused."[74]

These problems have encouraged some to propose modifications to standard TEE. For example, both Hovil and Holland have increased the emphasis on "spiritual formation" while Harrison's list of success factors includes the need to have a well-defined target audience.[75] Indeed, several prominent practitioners welcome a "significant shift away from the polarization" between a narrow definition of TEE towards what might be called "Diversified Theological Education" or "Integrated Leadership Development."[76] With TEE principles still preeminent, this approach advocates more emphasis on tailoring the program for the particular context, with the potential inclusion of elements such as bigger training conferences, and integration with partner colleges.[77] These two additional elements were therefore added to the study's "Alternative Methods" model" for preacher training (see Appendix A, "Alternative Methods").

Training Needs

Applying such a diversified approach to theological education requires recognition that the form of theological training is as important as its content; something Hovil identified during his time in Uganda.[78] At the core of his "dynamic curriculum development model," Hovil adopts three "planning grids" from Young ("structure," "curriculum" and "pedagogy") and adds a fourth: "context."[79] However, given the emphasis Young places on the user organisation having "a clearly defined goal based upon the identification of a specific leadership need," I added a fifth planning grid for "goals" that interrogates how well established an organisation's training goals are, and how well they are integrated into the organisation's strategy.[80] This five-dimensional "planning grid" formed a key part of my evaluation of ZEC's training needs. I also recognised that my evaluation framework could use elements of this model to characterise a user organisation's context and training needs as well as characterise a provider organisation's training program (see Appendix A, "ZEC Context Profile" and "Training Profile").

Hovil also reminds us of Costa's classification of particular theological educational goals as a balance between: to form (character, abilities, and thought); to inform (mind, praxis, and contemplation); and to transform (values, people, institutions and communities).[81] I also adopted this "Goals Model" into the analytical framework I used for my study (see Appendix A, "Goals").

Training Principles

Usefully, Hovil went on to distil his experience and perspective on the literature into several key "principles" and "components" required if a diversified theological program was to be effective.[82] I have synthesised Hovil's ideas with the broader literature (especially the overview of Harrison) to establish a framework of ten training principles for effective grassroots preacher training. [83]

First there must be careful contextualisation in four aspects of theological training, that is:

(1) the theology being taught;[84]

(2) the hermeneutic method being taught;[85]

(3) the homiletic method being taught;[86]

(4) the training method itself.[87]

Then six further areas must be carefully addressed:

(5) the scalability of the training method so sufficient numbers of grassroots preachers can be trained;[88]

(6) the sustainability of the program within the context so it is readily affordable by the community without external inputs;[89]

(7) the use of the Bible as the key course text so unsustainably expensive course material is avoided;[90]

(8) a focus on training preachers in practical skills;[91]

(9) the use of coaching/discipleship principles in the training;[92] and

(10) explicitly designing multiplication into the program so scalability is achieved through trainers being able to train trainers.[93]

These principles identified within Diversified Theology Education were incorporated as a further framework to characterise the training needs of the user organisation and the training delivered by provider organisations (see Appendix A, "Principles").

Coaching

Since the 1980s, especially in the USA and the UK, coaching and mentoring approaches to training began to be heavily used in corporate and public organisations.[94] These methods exhibit many similarities with the "discipleship" methods espoused by diversified theology, are increasingly used in the Western church context, and appear to present useful analytical frameworks for our study.[95]

First, while there is much debate over definitions,[96] and all involve "a relationship that promotes learning from experience in one or both partners,"[97] a useful distinction is generally made between broader "mentoring," (which covers "psycho-social" character development, and allows the mentor to "impart their own experience")[98] "coaching," (with a narrower focus on skills/competencies for a particular role, and relying on the coached to "learn for themselves")[99] and "discipling" (concentrated on "biblical truth and spiritual disciplines.") It might be argued all three are applicable in the context of undertrained and under-discipled grassroots preachers.

In addition, many of the specific techniques of coaching (such as active listening and the "GROW" model) would also appear applicable to the facilitation of alternative theological training models.[100] The claimed benefits also align with the objectives of diversified theological education, such as improved skills, reaching the unreached and helping people feel valued.[101] Identified success factors also seem to align with those identified for DTE (including: choosing and training the right people as coaches, allowing for cultural learning styles).[102]

However, the most powerful insight in the subject of mentoring is arguably that of Hunt and Weintraub, who highlighted the need for an appropriate organisational culture if mentor/coach-like training models are to succeed. With minor adaption, their work suggested that the leadership culture of ZEC could be usefully profiled using the following questions:

(1) Do leaders trust each other?
(2) Are leaders valued?
(3) Are relationships valued?
(4) Is learning valued?
(5) Are leaders encouraged to seek guidance?
(6) Is diversity of thought valued?
(7) Is innovation valued?
(8) Is continuous improvement valued?[103]

Once again, the lessons from another source of knowledge would appear to make a valuable contribution to an analytical framework to address the primary research question of this study (see Appendix A, "ZEC Leadership Culture").

Franchise Management

Perhaps a more controversial source of insight into viable grassroots theological education are the lessons from franchise management. These business techniques emerged in the second half of the last century as a "powerful new way of facilitating the growth of service organisations."[104] Humanly speaking, alternative training programs are services too, and they also have similar needs: to grow rapidly with limited resources in situations where local knowledge is critical.[105]

This area of knowledge appears to provide additional insights, but also re-enforces lessons from the other sources to suggest a framework of critical success factors.

For example, the fact that franchises are fundamentally interdependent partnerships between the franchisor and the franchisee makes it critical to select the right people, with the right motivation, to train them well, and to ensure ongoing training.[106] It is also clear that success depends on trust and shared goals, allowing the right balance between empowering entrepreneurial innovation and contextualisation (especially in a cross-cultural context) by the franchisee versus the need for the franchisor to control quality and brand.[107] Another common point is the need for the franchisor to have a robust and proven operating model that is simple enough to be easily taught to others.[108]

Church Planting and Multiplication

Over several decades, church planting movements around the world have used radical models that have demonstrated—at least to some degree—numerical scalability and economic sustainability in the majority world: so-called Church Planting and Multiplication (CPM).[109]

It is perhaps not surprising that many of the CPM principles align with those of TEE given their similar interest in building on the biblical principles of the early church.[110] Indeed, Patterson's influential work in Latin America explicitly built upon TEE to combine "pastoral training and evangelism in a church context."[111]

The TEE principles that are reinforced by CPM include the importance of contextualisation of content and method;[112] the importance of training the right people;[113] of training indigenous trainers;[114] the use of "on the job" coaching and mentoring techniques;[115] a focus on training elders;[116] and avoidance of dependence on the West.

However, CPM also appears to bring a far greater focus than TEE would typically do on building into the "DNA" of its models the use of very simple, reproducible, materials to equip every trainer to be quickly released to train trainers themselves.[117] Hence, traditional arithmetic growth of trained leaders can—at least in principle—become geometric.[118] Such training movements bring their own leadership challenges, especially if they are unsympathetically imposed on local cultures, and it is arguable that they rarely fully demonstrate their claimed potential. However, they bring the possibility of grassroots leader training closer to the form of multiplicative apostolic succession seen in 2 Tim 2:2.[119]

The things which you have heard from me in the presence of many witnesses, entrust these to faithful men who will be able to teach others also.
(2 Tim 2:2)

So, Diversified Theological Education has allowed me to create potentially useful models for the characterisation of the perceived needs for grassroots preacher training, and the principles applied to such training. Then perspectives appropriated from the realm of executive coaching were not only found to support these models but also allowed us to build a framework to evaluate the readiness of ZEC's leadership culture for alternative training models. Similarly, while again re-enforcing the earlier work, the very different knowledge domains of franchise management and church planting brought even greater emphasis on reproducibility and scalability.

This now, finally, allows me to aggregate the various perspectives from these "other sources" into a tentative model of Critical Success Factors (CSF) for preacher training programs: (1) training sufficient trainers; (2) selecting the right trainers; (3) empowering trainers to innovate; (4) empowering trainers to train trainers; (5) ensuring ongoing training and coaching; (6) focussing on character formation; (7) developing contextually appropriate methods; (8) keep methods simple, low-cost and reproducible; (9) focus on who is being trained; (10) empowering local leaders to contextualise the program; and (11) integrate into the overall strategy of the local church (see Appendix A, "Critical Success Factors").

Conclusions on Conceptual Framework

The appropriate literature appears to support the premise of the primary research question concerning contextualisation, scalability and sustainability being important dimensions of my analysis. This has allowed me to build a rich, and potentially useful, framework which has formed the basis of my qualitative and quantitative analysis of grassroots preacher training in ZEC.

My work also raises several secondary research questions. Chiefly, does my case study validate: the problems with preaching in rural sub-Saharan Africa, and the problems with traditional approaches to preacher training; both of which are identified in the literature? Does it also validate the assumed priority for preacher training in rural sub-Saharan Africa, and the importance of contextualising "what" (theology, hermeneutics, homiletics) and "how" (methodology) preachers are trained in rural sub-Saharan Africa?

Moreover, does the field work I have used demonstrate any merit in the derived analytical framework, methods, and tools as an approach to evaluating alternatives for preacher training in other contexts within sub-Saharan Africa?

Finally, it must be assessed if, as a result of my research, any recommendations can be made, initially for ZEC in rural Malawi, but also for providers of preacher training in rural sub-Saharan Africa and churches in search of preacher training that context.

Chapter 2: Evaluating Effectiveness

I designed my field research project with the above conceptual framework, and the clearly defined research questions, using the approach of Thomas, augmented primarily by Robson.[120]

Design

Experience shows that my ontological assumptions are driven by my professional training as an engineer and my personal theology.[121] As a trained scientist I see reality as "both real and, in principle, accessible;" but this is balanced by an engineer's pragmatism and a theological understanding of a fallen world.[122] In other words, investigators might never have perfect knowledge, but they can get good enough knowledge for all practical purposes.[123]

Considering the broad topic of qualitative versus quantitative data gathering, my research questions appeared amenable to "nomothetic" and "ideographic" analysis, and I knew that "triangulation" would be critical in evaluating the effectiveness of the derived analytical framework.[124] I therefore resolved to use a "mixed methods" or "multiple methods" approach.[125]

Having reflected on my research questions, the scope/duration of the project, and my move to work with Zambesi Mission in Malawi, I concluded that I had a rare opportunity to carry out a detailed Case Study of an especially challenging environment for preaching and preacher training.[126] The primary case study could also be augmented with aspects of a Cross-Sectional Study by segmenting the users' groups within ZEC, and with aspects of a Comparative Study by comparing and contrasting organisations providing training.[127]

In all this it was clear that the necessarily limited scope of the project would eliminate any statistical significance of the data I collected.[128]

Ethics

I judged there to be a low probability of low level harm occurring to participants. Nevertheless, while the various training program executives to be interviewed could not be considered "vulnerable," I offered anonymity to the individuals involved and their organisations.[129]

I also recognised that the indigenous participants might feel vulnerable about damage to their "standing or reputation" within the "community" of Zambezi Evangelical Church through their participation.[130] Hence, these participants were also protected through anonymity and file encryption. As a final safeguard, all parties were also given the opportunity to withdraw their data from the study at any time.

As a Western missionary with the support of ZEC's General Secretary, I would inevitably have significant contextual power. I therefore operated an explicit opt-in process that recorded the voluntary informed consent of all participants.

Methods

Having decided on my design-frame, and considered the ethical considerations of my research, it became apparent that a Survey approach would best meet my objective of integrating qualitative and quantitative methods.[131] Qualitative data would bring richness and depth, quantitative data would aid comparison of different segments, while triangulation, and in particular methodological triangulation, would allow a tentative validation of the analytical framework being used to evaluate training needs and training solutions.[132]

Semi-Structured Interview

After reviewing the options, I decided on a semi-structured interview to gather rich qualitative data from users of training and providers of training.[133] This would provide "the best of both worlds" combining a structured list with the "freedom to follow up points as necessary."[134] For each class of participants, I constructed a series of questions based on the key areas of investigation relevant to their roles.[135]

I was careful to minimise experimental effects such as experimenter expectancy by starting with an open question before asking a more leading question. This was particularly important for grassroots indigenous leaders where my perceived contextual power might encourage them to seek the answer they thought I wanted.

Guided Questionnaire

In addition to the interview questions, I prepared a more quantitative questionnaire based on the key characteristics of the derived analytical framework, with the aim of providing more quantitative data to facilitate analysis and comparison.[136] The questions broadly followed the same high-level structure as the interview and mainly used two formats of question, the "semantic differential scale" and "matrix questions."[137]

To ensure data quality, I decided to guide research partners through the questionnaire while working hard to minimise experimenter expectancy. One way I did this was to mix the polarity of the questions to avoid the interviewee anticipating the answer they thought I desired.

Existing Document Analysis

To gain another perspective on the approach of leader/preacher training programs, and to gain further rich qualitative information, I asked the training provider organisations that I interviewed to give me sample policy documents and course material. Based on prior research experience I decided to carry out "document interrogation" using a simple form of "thick description" using a coding model based on the analytical framework.[138]

Self-Guided Survey

A second questionnaire was used to survey a wider sample of grassroots preachers (elders and pastors) to gain a broader understanding of their situation, and perspectives on user needs.

The survey questions were designed to be self-guided, to use simple unambiguous language, and to predominantly use closed questions to elicit data more readily analysed quantitatively. However, I also asked more open questions on the participant's most recent sermon to obtain qualitative information on sermon style.

The survey was translated into Chichewa by a bi-lingual church leader, proofread by a professional translator and tested with bilingual Malawian Christians of different educational backgrounds.

Learning Styles

As discussed above, despite the obvious limitations of using such a complex tool in rural Africa, I decided to follow Howles and use the Learning Styles Questionnaire (LSQ) to analyse the learning styles of preachers in ZEC.[139] I did not attempt to simplify the English of the official 40-question LSQ, but aimed to keep the Chichewa as simple as possible.

Process

Care was taken to ensure that a significant number of research partners from the grassroots user community were selected from the (approximately) 80% of ZEC leaders (and Malawi citizens) who live and work in rural environments. However, I decided to choose research partners from the Central and Southern region of Malawi only. These regions comprise approximately 90% of the membership of ZEC, and it was judged this more limited geographic scope would reduce communications challenges without compromising the validity of the results.

Interview and Guided Questionnaire of Users

To produce a good cross-sectional analysis of ZEC, three representatives from four "layers" in the organisation were interviewed: (1) church elders, (2) church pastors, (3) regional leaders, and (4) national leaders.

All user interviews were carried out face-to-face, targeted to take 90 minutes, and recorded to leave me free to concentrate on facilitating the discussion. When the interviewee felt it helpful, I used a Chichewa/English interpreter for the interview. The same interpreter was used for all interviews and was a ZEC theology undergraduate considered able to understand the subject matter, but without enough "contextual authority" to risk distorting the interview.

Interview and Guided Questionnaire of Providers

Provider organisations were selected in two categories: (1) Three "existing programs" (E1–E3) were selected from the four church leadership training programs already active in some way with ZEC members and churches. (2) Four "potential programs" (P1–P4) were selected from many well-established preacher training programs that were active in sub-Saharan Africa. This stratification of the provider sample was expected to allow useful cross-sectional analysis between existing and potential training providers.[140]

The provider interviews were carried out face-to-face or via Skype video calls. Both methods were judged to give equally good results. In general, the interview was with a senior board-level executive of the organisation.

Again, the interview was recorded to leave me free to concentrate on facilitating the discussion and to allow later transcription of the interview. Again, the interview was targeted to take 90 minutes but was typically longer because of the enthusiasm of the participants. Everyone interviewed was asked to provide additional written material giving further insight into the goals, principles, content, and methods of the training program. All did so.

Self-Guided Survey

The limitations of postal and email communications meant that the self-guided survey had to be distributed in person through regional governance meetings (the "Kotale" or district presbytery meeting every quarter) that gather the pastor and representative elders from churches in a local area. I randomly selected three Kotales: two from the Southern region and one from the Central region, to provide approximately 80 returns across pastors and elders from predominantly rural areas. While this could not be considered as providing a statistically significant sample, the considerable volume of quantitative data would add real value to the qualitative data gathered from the interviews. The chairmen of two Kotale were briefed face-to-face on administering the survey. I conducted the third survey myself.

Chapter 3: Analysing ZEC

Analytical Tools

Wherever possible, simple, readily understood, analytical tools were used for both quantitative and qualitative data.

Quantitative

I analysed the quantitative information gathered in my study using standard statistical analysis (e.g. modes, means, standard deviations) and graphical inspection, while "learning style" and "preaching style" data required more sophisticated analysis. Throughout, it was understood that the limited sample sizes achievable in this study meant that data would not be strictly statistically significant.[141]

Wherever relevant, the analysis made distinctions in the results of the main strata in the samples to aid cross-sectional analysis between, for example, pastors/elders or existing/potential training programs.[142]

Qualitative

Over 30 hours of interviews were transcribed across 14 user interviews and 7 provider interviews. Given the resources available, a simple form of "thick description" analytical approach was used together with a very simple coding model related to the analytical framework.[143] Coded text was then added to a tabular form of "data display" for ease of cross-referencing against quantitative data.[144] While not all interviews produced data on all areas of study, in aggregate the interviews provided a comprehensive dataset.

Document analysis of the material supplied by provider organisations was analysed in the same way, and key information added to the display table. Finally, a comprehensive summary report was produced for each provider.

Triangulation and Comparison

Quantitative/qualitative data and user/provider data was structured against the common analytical framework. The former facilitates triangulation; the latter facilitates the comparison of user needs and provider characteristics, and both drove the discussion and recommendations in subsequent chapters.

User Results and Analysis

ZEC Research Partners

My primary research of ZEC as a user of preacher training gathered a wealth of rich data from 12 semi-structured interviews and a survey of 82 ZEC preachers.

Results from the survey showed several issues with the methods used. The questions requiring qualitative answers were frequently skipped, and the semantic difference scale questions appeared difficult for people in a rural context to understand. Several questions also showed a degree of "noise" in the results, which suggests that people had difficulty interpreting the questions. For example, when it came to declaring the number of members in their "church" some were unclear whether this should include the main "parent church" and all its "prayer houses," or just the "parent church" or just their local "prayer house."

Nevertheless, the researched group proved usefully representative of ZEC as a whole (even if not a true statistically significant sample) with elders making up 72% of the researched group, and 84% of the group being from rural areas.

ZEC Context

In terms of the national context, research partners report Malawi to be a culturally Christian country with "a long-time history of Christianity," but with a "very shallow" understanding of what "Christianity is all about," and where the church is losing trust. Secularism is seen to be "creeping in," creating a materialism that sees Christianity as "for the poor," is transforming society so that some feel they live in a "foreign country," and re-enforcing a dependency "syndrome."

Quantitative results from church executives (see Appendix B, Fig. B1) showed considerable variation but broadly evaluate the ZEC "context and culture" as relatively low in resource ("Frankly speaking ZEC economically is very very poor"), primarily rural, and generally balanced between formal/informal and centralised/decentralised organisational models. While ZEC is recognised as a vibrant gospel centred church, qualitatively the executives report significant spiritual challenges within the church including syncretism ("We combine Christian and traditional cultural ideas in the church, which is not good") and nominalism. Low education standards ("pathetic" literacy rates quoted as "60–65% functionally illiterate") and a significant proportion of elders who are "not real Christians" and who simply "cause conflict," exacerbates these challenges; as does quantitative data indicating a leadership culture with weaknesses in trust, openness, and commitment to learning (see Appendix B, Fig. B2). Some see this resulting in "a church without purpose or vision" and still running on the traditional lines "of our forefathers."

ZEC Churches

Churches in the surveyed group varied considerably in size (see Appendix B, Fig. B3). The largest had over 1,000 members, and urban churches tended to be larger than rural (with a mode of 300-500 compared to 200-300). There was also a wide variation in the number of elders per membership (with a mean of 17 members per elder) and giving per member; with the mode for rural churches being less than 10 MwK (approx. £0.02 at the time of study) per member per week.

The ZEC churches also have a complex distributed form, with rural churches having a mean of 4 "prayer houses" (see Appendix A, Fig. B4) that are often large; 40% of rural prayer houses in the sample had 100–199 members. These satellite churches are located an average of 1.5 hrs walk from the main church (see Appendix A, Fig. B5), in a context where a third of the church leaders have no form of transport and almost all the rest rely on a bicycle.

ZEC Preachers

Preachers surveyed ranged in age from 25 to 74, with a mean of 47 years old (see Appendix B, Fig. B6), and over 30% of the elders had only attended primary school while 86% had no education beyond school (see Appendix B, Fig. B7). All pastors and most elders (93%)

surveyed owned a Bible, with 75% of preachers (81% of elders) exclusively using a Chichewa Bible and a similar proportion (80% of preachers) reporting Chichewa as the only language they were comfortable reading.

Most of the surveyed preachers (69%) have mobile phones while only 10% have smartphones and 5% computers with the potential for internet connectivity. So, FM radio (accessible on most phones and TVs in Malawi) is the ubiquitous electronic communication medium (see Appendix A, Fig. B8).

ZEC Preaching

Both the elders and the pastors interviewed saw preaching as "really important". It is seen to be important on theological grounds because it is the "only way by which an individual can be brought into fuller experience of the Word of God" such that "you cannot exclude preaching from the life of the church." However, in the oral culture of rural Malawi, preaching is an especially authoritative medium, where illiteracy means "most of them depend on hearing the Word," and a lack of a Bible study culture means that as a church leader "the only opportunity that God gives you [to teach] is the Sunday service that you preach."

All who were interviewed reported significant problems with preaching within ZEC, and with rural preaching by church elders who give about 70–80% of the sermons each Sunday without necessarily having calling, gifting, or passion: "Many elders are being elected [and expected to preach] but they don't have the gift, calling, or passion for preaching." A situation was described where a lack of training means sermons are often second hand, based on an isolated verse taken out of context, with the passage possibly even treated as a parable when it is history: "many preach from a short verse with no context and turn into a parable what is actually a bit of history." In addition, many will preach a favourite passage regardless of the topic or their favourite subject irrespective of the passage, struggle to find a theme and application faithful to scripture, and hence create a sermon that is "not truly grounded in the Word of God," possibly full of traditional stories contrary to scripture, and having no coherence:

"some cannot preach without telling a [traditional proverb style] story about a hare, that is not even associated with the passage."

Quantitative survey data adds to this picture of preaching within ZEC with an elder typically preaching one or two times a month (see Appendix B, Fig. B9), to an average of 140 people (see Appendix B, Fig. 10), and preaching to different congregations within the "station" led by the pastor. Only 41% of pastors decide what to preach based on a Bible verse or passage, with others selecting a topic or perceived congregational need or being influenced through, for example, prayer (see Appendix B, Fig. B11). Moreover, they aim to address a broad range of perceived spiritual challenges including nominalism, spiritual immaturity, polygamy, syncretism with African traditional religion, and other issues. A large proportion (32%) of the elders spend less than an hour preparing these sermons while 92% spend less than 4 hours, and almost all (78%) use nothing except their Bible to prepare. Most then make sermon notes (94%) but in the majority of cases these are just headings.

ZEC Learning Styles

The learning style preferences of ZEC preachers was evaluated using the model (as described in Chapter 2,) which is based on the work of Honey and Mumford, with all the pastors and elders interviewed or surveyed being asked the forty diagnostic question.[145] In context, many research partners found answering these questions a challenge, but useful data was obtained from approx. 60% of the questionnaires.

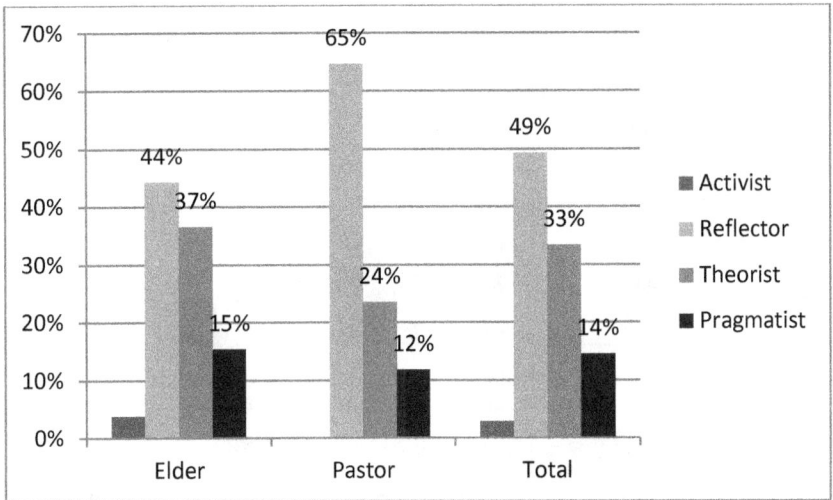

Fig. 2 – Learning Style Preference

The questions were carefully analysed to determine which learning style the research partners preferred. The most common preference (see Fig. 2 above) was Reflector (49%), followed by Theorist (33%). There is also an indication that pastors might have a higher propensity to have a Reflector preference than elders (65% versus 44%).

Most research partners (75%) showed only a single learning preference, although there was an indication that pastors were more likely than elders to have a single preference.

ZEC Preaching Styles

The preaching style of ZEC was evaluated using the Homiletic Window model described in Chapter 2, with the pastors and elders who were interviewed or surveyed being asked nine diagnostic questions concerning the "function" and "form" of the sermon (see Appendix A, "Preaching"). Many research partners found answering these semantic differential questions a challenge, but useful data was obtained from approx. 60% of the questionnaires.

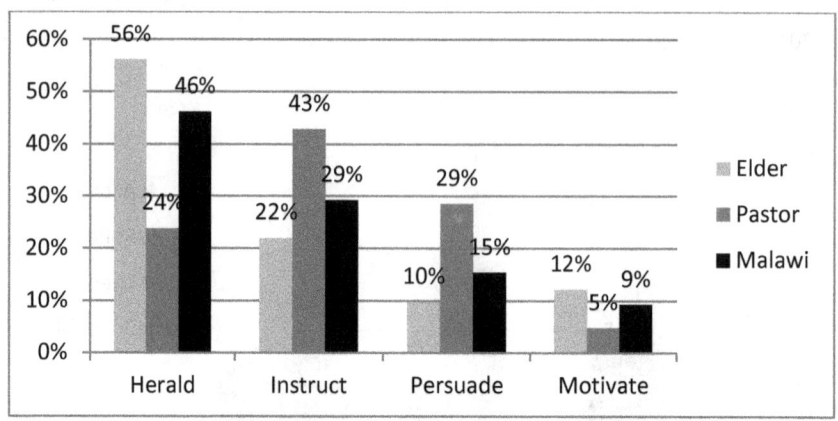

Fig. 3 – Preaching Style Preference

The questions were carefully analysed (see Fig. 3, above) to determine which preaching style the research partners exhibited. All preaching styles in the Homiletic Window are represented in the results, but there is a greater propensity for elders to exhibit a "Herald" preaching style and pastors an "Instruct" style. This was consistent with other survey data (see Appendix B, Fig. B11) that found that pastors appeared more influenced by perceived congregational needs than a specific Bible passage in choosing their sermon topic, with elders it was the other way around. Unfortunately, qualitative data from the survey concerning the preacher's last sermon was sparse and gave little diagnostic information on the preachers' views on the function and preferred form of a sermon.

ZEC Perspectives on Preacher Training

All strata in the organisation recognised alternative approaches to preacher training as "very important indeed" for training elders and retraining pastors. One elder put it succinctly: "[F]or us elders to preach the Word of God we need to be taught how to preach."

ZEC executives recognised real problems with traditional methods of preacher training such as residential colleges; that they don't train enough people or the right people (see Appendix B, Fig. B12). The surveyed and interviewed preachers put this in context. While all pastors said they had received some form of preacher training, over half (56%) of elders said they had received no training. Of the rest of the elders, the majority had been on one-off short courses of a few days duration (e.g. "elders training – one day") held many years ago, and those were typically not specifically about preaching (e.g. "This training was mostly centred on church management.") Nevertheless, most of those who had received such training had a strong recollection of the principles.

In terms of high-level program design, the executives gave surprisingly high results that recognised the importance of all the components presented in the literature (e.g. home study, seminars). However, they rated training conferences significantly less important than the others (see Appendix B, Fig. B13). In turn, when asked about high-level training goals, they saw all three goals as important; i.e. training that formed and informed the individual and transformed the community (see Appendix B, Fig. B15). However, they also recognised that their goals were ill-defined and lacked integration within an overall ZEC strategy (see Appendix B, Fig. B1).

When it came to more detailed training needs, the executives had a variety of views but quantitative (see Appendix B, Fig. B14) and qualitative data indicated a broad need for training that is more formal than informal, decentralised to Kotale level (e.g. "I prefer a structure based at quarterly level ... to minimise travelling expenses,") with an applied curriculum that is highly targeted at grassroots preachers, and a curriculum inclined towards an involved and discovery oriented methodology (e.g. "In a rural setting like this one, for people ... to learn something they need to be involved as well.")

The executives also confirmed as important all the principles for viable alternative training methods identified in the evaluation framework, with the need to be "Bible centric" and to support "explicit multiplication" seen as the most significant of all (Appendix B, Fig. B15).

The survey group gave a wide range of answers about what topics they would like to see in the curriculum. Over 60% of responses related to Bible knowledge, hermeneutics, and homiletics (e.g. "How to preach," "Sermon preparation," "Understanding the Bible," "How to find the subject and points for the sermon.") Most of the rest requested training in areas of specific theological importance within the context (e.g. "tithing" or "repentance") and in general leadership (e.g. "church administration.") Comments during interviews supported this trend (e.g. "you have to learn to interpret [Scripture] and you have to learn to apply it") while also emphasising the need for developing people's personal faith (e.g. "[I would like] topics to do with my life ... holiness, love.")

Concerning the time and money that grassroots preachers could commit to such training, the survey and interview data was difficult to interpret. However, there appeared to be a consensus that it would be possible to meet once or twice a month for a local study group (e.g. "Maybe two times a month. That can work ... of an hour and a half"), and 3–5 days for a bigger, less regular seminar type event (e.g. "We can be at the training 3 or 4 days in a week.") Similarly, there might be a rough consensus at around 1–2,000 MwK per person per month for local training and perhaps 10–20,000 MwK for the bigger and less frequent events.

Provider Results and Analysis

Provider Research Partners

The training organisations that I analysed included three existing programs already active in Malawi (E1–E3) and four potential programs (P1–P4) active in Africa but not yet in Malawi. For a high-level profile of these programs see Appendix B, Fig. B16.

Of the three existing programs, already active with ZEC, E1 is a well-established global program with a Malawian in local leadership. E2 is a Malawi-tailored program with a European local leader. E3 is a new program focussed on Malawi and led by joint UK/Malawi leaders. All make extensive or exclusive use of local trainers.

Of the "Potential Programs" interviewed P1, P2 and P3 are run by global agencies headquartered in the US or UK. They operate (at least initially) with Western trainers flying in for week-long events. P4 is developed by Africans for Africa with local trainers, although curriculum coordination is now UK based.

ZEC and Africa Context

The training providers interviewed confirmed the contextual information in the literature. In particular, they identified key issues including inadequate education levels in the churches, low levels of spiritual maturity, character and training issues with elders ("They lack adequate Bible training and the study materials required to understand and preach the Word of God effectively"), poor preaching, and an inherent culture of clericalism, syncretism ("They are also faced with ... longstanding inherited tribal beliefs,") and dependency ("Africa tends to have a default setting of 'You ought to be helping me.'")

Existing programs were also able to profile ZEC's specific context (see Appendix B, Fig B17), judging that ZEC's preacher training goals were ill-defined and not integrated into an overall strategy, that their ministry was overwhelmingly rural, and was carried out with little resource within a rather confused organisational structure: "[ZEC] wants officially to be a formal organisation" but in the end, it's an informal process dominated by personal rather than formal relationships.

Importance of Preaching and Preacher Training

Providers unanimously espoused the critical importance of preaching in an oral context like rural Malawi where there are few Bibles available and few church members who can read them. One provider remarked: "How are people learning the Word? It's through preaching, word of mouth mainly."

Similarly, there was a universal understanding of the importance of grassroots preacher training, with one declaring: "I couldn't over-emphasise it." In this respect elders needed to be the "first target group," to be helped to understand "Biblical eldership," and to become proficient in "hermeneutics and homiletics," and in "expository preaching." This is particularly important in a ZEC context where it is only pastors who have "had a chance to go for Bible training," and leaving many prayer houses with "nobody trained to deliver the preaching."

Evaluating Training Methods

All the training providers interviewed (see Appendix B, Fig. B18) confirmed that "traditional" residential college-type training methods failed to train enough people, train the right people, or (to a lesser extent) train people in the right things.

Concerning their views on the key components of "alternative" training methods, there was again broad consensus (see Appendix B, B19) that "college integration" and "home study" are relatively low in importance compared to "practical ministry" and "seminars." Considering "home study," one provider judged that "it's got to be more than just a guy sitting and trying to figure this out by himself," while thinking about "college integration" another felt it important for "[informal] leadership training to be accepted [and valued] for what it is" rather than a route to more formal education.

Program Profiles, Goals and Principles

There was considerable variation in the self-perception of individual programs in terms of profiling their practice against context, structure, curriculum, and methodology (see Appendix B, Fig B20). Most potential programs saw themselves as well matched to a low-resource context, and all programs considered they had an application oriented curriculum matched to grassroots needs. However, their appropriateness for rural environments and their methodologies vary more significantly. The implication of these variations on the suitability of individual programs against the needs of ZEC will be discussed in the next chapter.

Similarly, there was an interesting variation (see Appendix B, Fig. B21) in the perceived importance of the different "goals" of preacher training. One program rated "to inform" particularly low, as their focus was on changing practice, while another rated "to transform" very low. Again, it was felt important to emphasise that programs are "not training you to become a pastor."

When it came to the "principles" of alternative approaches to preacher training, in general the "potential programs" rated themselves lower (see Appendix B, Fig. B22) than "existing programs" in their ability to meet the principles. Some considered themselves particularly weak at contextualising the theology and hermeneutic methods they teach, and how integral coaching/discipleship is to their methodology.

Almost all programs were already aware of their perceived weaknesses in these areas of principle and practice and had active programs in place to improve matters.

Program Approach to Preaching

All programs gave considerable prominence to preaching, but there was a variation in the preaching preferences derived from the quantitative analysis of their preferences against the Homiletic Window model (See Fig. 4 below). While each of the existing programs presented a different preaching preference, three out of four of the potential programs indicated at least an implicit norm of "Herald" was presented within their training program. The preference most commonly associated in the literature with the West.

Herald	E3, P1, P2, P4
Instruct	
Persuade	E2
Motivate	E1, P3

Fig. 4 – Program Preaching Norms

In contrast to these quantitative results, the qualitative data from interviews shows most potential programs arguing that they do not promote a particular preaching norm. They claimed to be "not that specific in terms of style and approach," to "back it up one step and talk about normative preaching being expositional in nature," to recognise the fallacy of thinking that "what persuades us as Westerners, a linear deductive argument … will persuade Africans," and the reality that "[sermon] form is cultural."

Perhaps the strong "Herald" results are driven by implicit Western preaching norms that some programs recognised as "a big issue" and has led at least two programs (P2 and P3) to reconsider their "[homiletic] methodology that doesn't work in grassroots majority world contexts."

Program and Critical Success Factors

Once again, there was considerable variation in the perspective that different programs had on their match against the derived "Critical Success Factors" for effective grassroots preacher training (See Appendix B, Fig. B23). However, all the existing programs rated themselves highly concerning their ability to focus on their target audience and target message, as did the potential programs who also consistently rated themselves highly for empowering trainers to train trainers. Equally there was no consistent weakness identified by the existing programs, while the potential programs consistently identified their weakness at empowering trainers to innovate within their local context.

Chapter 4: Discussing ZEC

ZEC Context

Briefly reflecting on the context, the main thing to observe is the broad consensus between the perspectives of the three constituencies involved in this study (the perspectives of the literature, the ZEC users and the training program providers) concerning ZEC: that, humanly speaking, Malawi is one of the most challenging contexts in sub-Saharan Africa for any form of church development.

Economically, the nation lies at the bottom of the tables of almost every key index. Socially, secularism and materialism are beginning to turn the people away from a century of Christian heritage. Spiritually, as people increasingly aspire to Western "success," conservative evangelical Christianity (e.g. not including the so called "prosperity gospel") is seen as "something only for the poor."

In this national situation, ZEC finds itself particularly challenged economically ("ZEC economically is very very poor") with no significant denominational support from the West, and a demographic dominated by rural subsistence farmers giving on average less than £0.02 per member per month to the church. It is also challenged spiritually with, for example, widespread nominalism and syncretism.

Having said all this, it is interesting to note the significant variation of views among ZEC executives and the representatives of existing programs concerning the resource levels within ZEC (See Appendix B, Fig. B1). I interpret this as reflecting that, while many church members have a "begging kind of syndrome," national leaders recognise the considerable latent human resource in the membership that, with the right approach, might be usefully deployed.

Similarly, the range of views concerning the structure of the church could be interpreted as reflecting a healthy balance between formal processes and informal communication, and seems to reflect the mid-level Kotale as a powerhouse in the organisation.

So, despite the challenging context there appear to be opportunities for ZEC: an organisation with a strong, Bible centred, heritage of self-reliance; a political environment that provides a relatively peaceful and stable society that continues to be broadly supportive of the Christian message; a clear centre for mobilisation in the Kotale, and an indication of untapped human resource to be mobilised.

So, while an objective of establishing sustainable preacher training within Malawi in general, and specifically within ZEC, might be particularly challenging, the context certainly does not rule it out entirely. Equally, if methods can be discovered that are viable in this context, they will almost certainly be viable elsewhere in sub-Saharan Africa.

ZEC Preaching

Importance and Nature of Preaching

Considering the debate in the literature on the topic, it was important to consider whether the presupposition that preaching is truly important holds true in the context of my study. It is therefore important to note that both user and provider results confirmed this. However, for a Western audience it is perhaps the emphasis on the practical importance of preaching within the context that is of greatest import: it is the *spoken* word (not the written word) that is uniquely effective and authoritative in the orality and functional illiteracy of Malawi. As I have already mentioned, one training program representative starkly put it: "How are people learning the Word? It's through preaching."

It is equally important (if perhaps not surprising giving its faith heritage) to recognise that ZEC also appears to affirm—at least in principle—the presupposition that preaching is fundamentally expository in nature; with one preacher saying preaching was "expounding the Word of God" to plant "the Word of God in their [the congregation's] hearts." Unsurprisingly this also aligns with all the training programs which typically see their objective as "to bring [preachers] back to expository preaching" which is "preaching what the Bible is saying."

Problems with Preaching

As well as a consensus concerning the importance of preaching, the primary research also showed a consensus on the problems with preaching within ZEC, which in turn reflects and validates the issues referenced in the literature concerning sub-Saharan Africa.

It is also important to note the scale of the impact these problems have on the church, something made clear by the evidence that each church has an average of 4 prayer houses resulting in 70–80% of sermons being by elders. What is more, the average size of a congregation served by an elder is approximately 140, certainly not small by UK standards.

It is also important to flag the key root causes of these problems that were observed during the study of ZEC.

First, a preacher can lack vocation. There is repeated reference by ZEC interviewees to the tradition that elders are voted into post rather than appointed, and they are then almost always expected to preach regardless of spiritual maturity or gifting: "Many people are being voted but they don't have that gift of preaching, the calling itself, the passion itself."

Second, there is a multitude of practical difficulties for the preachers who have few books, limited transport, and limited telecommunications. Thus constrained, they are asked to preach approximately twice a month to different congregations located several hours walk from the main church.

Finally, there is the lack of education and training, with 31% of elders having only primary education, only 18% able to read English language materials, and over half the elders being untrained — and the rest undertrained — in preaching.

Opportunities

Despite these oft stated problems, the ZEC preaching context also appears to show some real opportunities for improving preaching.

At its most fundamental this is seen in the fact that the priority of the church is to "[t]each God's word," even if many struggle to understand and communicate its message. In addition, while access to Bibles is a major problem across sub-Saharan churches, almost all ZEC elders surveyed (93%) had access to a Bible in their preferred language. The preachers are also, for the culture, relatively young (the mode was 40–45 years) and, like their senior leaders, see preaching and preacher training as a priority. Further, while they have received little or no training on preaching, it is also clear that any training received has been valued and remembered over many years. The fact that all pastors having received some form of preacher training—typically at undergraduate Certificate or Diploma level—is also a relatively strong position compared to many African Independent Churches and provides a potential foundation for local trainers/coaches. And, finally, while it may be surprising to a Western audience, the average 4:1 ratio of prayer houses to main churches is significantly lower than some larger Malawi denominations.[146]

ZEC Learning Style

Of the many models of learning preferences that have been developed, the two most established are the 1950s vintage "field dependency" model of Witkin, and the 1970s vintage Kolb Learning Style Inventory (LSI).[147]

Despite the previously mentioned debate over the influence of culture on learning preferences, there appears to be broad consensus that sub-Saharan Africans generally have a cultural propensity for "field dependent" (rather than "field independent") characteristics such as an emphasis on group cooperation, cultural imagery, and verbal tasks.[148] Although this was not directly tested in this study, this conclusion in the literature does appear to be validated by the interviewees and related literature on sub-Saharan preachers. For example: Chifungo recognises the typical learning style as "empathetic and participatory,"[149] Nhiwatiwa highlights the use of "pictorial language,"[150] a ZEC executive reflected that most Malawians "like discussion as a group and sharing ideas," and at least one of the training programs intentionally applies "what we see in the villages—people sitting around in groups and talking."

However, as mentioned earlier, my study directly evaluated learning styles and, while it is clear from the literature that we should not necessarily expect a correlation at the level of the individual between the nature of an individual's field-dependence and their learning style,[151] the results do appear to give interesting insight relevant to the contextualisation of preacher training.

Once again it should be noted that my study's methodology was based on a derivative model by Honey and Mumford (LSQ) rather than Kolb's LSI model itself. As previously mentioned, using LSQ rather than LSI allowed direct comparison with rare work profiling sub-Saharan pastoral students by Howles, the use of a short 40 question tool, and the use of more concrete, context-friendly, questions.[152]

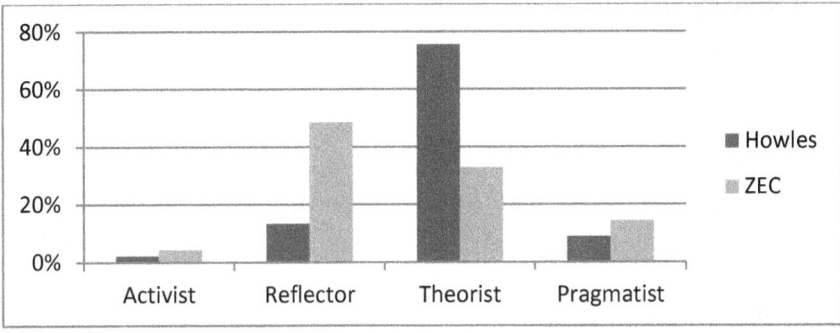

Fig. 5 – Sub-Saharan Learning Styles

A comparison between the results from this study ("ZEC" in Fig. 5 above) and that of Howles in Uganda shows a definite similarity.[153] It indicates that most preachers in at least two distinct sub-Saharan studies have "Reflector" or "Theorist" learning preferences. While such small samples cannot be considered conclusive, this does appear to be a clear indication of contextual learning style preference: "Reflectors" preferring to stand back, observe, and reflect; "Theorists" preferring to integrate observations into logical theories.[154]

However, even if proved to be a repeatable correlation, its application requires care. First, we must remember that the contextual association may be as much to do with the educational or professional specialism of preachers as to do with culture.[155] The preferences of general ZEC members might, therefore, be very different and, if alternative training methods were to broaden the background of preachers, then the profile might change. Second, the literature shows that the effectiveness of tailoring training based on learning style is questionable given the large variety of other parameters that can affect learning outcomes.[156] Third, trainers need to consider the preferences of all the individuals in a group, no matter how much of a minority. [157]

Some of the programs investigated showed an understanding of the need to address individual learning styles. Nevertheless, a generally increased awareness of learning styles would certainly appear beneficial, both for the development and the implementation of preacher training. Further, the recognition that—at least at present—most preachers are field dependent, reflectors and/or theorists could usefully be taken even more into account during course design.[158]

ZEC Preaching Style

As was mentioned previously, the interviews and survey data concerning the preacher's last sermon provided insufficient information for useful analysis. However, the little available appears to reflect expectations in the literature. For example, some preachers showed a clear propensity for inductive sermon forms (e.g. "Where possible I try to use stories," and "I use a song and a story,") while others apparently selected their sermon topic inductively (e.g. "I chose the message depending on the situation of the church right then.")

More interestingly, the quantitative analysis based on the Homiletic Window appears to provide useful insight into the nature of ZEC preaching. For, given the little qualitative information from the study and that from the literature, one might have predicted a preference for the "Persuade" preaching style within the model, where the function of the sermon is seen as that of the inductive "Pastor" and the form as that of the inductive "Poet."[159] Equally, with reports of trained pastors learning Western preaching norms while untrained/undertrained elders remain closer to their cultural roots, one might have expected pastors to have a higher propensity than elders to show a preference for the "Herald" style with the assumed function of deductive "Proclaimer" and form of deductive "Philosopher."

However, the empirical results are markedly different from this and show both pastors and elders indicating a preference for a deductive preaching form, and the less-trained elders rather than the trained pastors showing the stronger preference for the deductive "Proclaimer" perspective concerning the "function" of the sermon. Indeed, because elders do most of the preaching, it is the elders' "Herald" preaching style (traditionally considered a Western style) that would be expected to typify ZEC preaching compared to the "Instruct" style of the pastors. This divergence from received wisdom concerning African preaching clearly deserves further investigation.

Nevertheless, the distinction between elders and pastors in the perceived "function" of a sermon is supported by the separate data on what influences a preacher's choice of sermon topic. Here too, elders report a more deductive approach driven by a Bible passage and pastors a more inductive approach based on perceived congregational need.

Also of note, these trends could be broadly consistent with the study's results on learning styles. Anderson's original work means the Homiletic Window is directly related to Kolb's LSI model and hence to Honey and Mumford's LSQ model.[160] This might logically lead to a conclusion that the preponderance of Reflector/Theorist learning styles among ZEC preachers would imply a preponderance of Herald/Instruct preaching styles. However, significant work beyond the scope of this study would be required to be able to draw meaningful conclusions from this observation.

Nevertheless, even if necessarily tentative, these results do provide insights concerning preacher training in ZEC. First, for whatever reason and even if not quite in the way expected, elders and pastors appear to have different perspectives on preaching. A ZEC program would usefully take account of these different starting points.

Second, there may be a difference between the preacher's aspirations in preaching (as measured by the Homiletic Window) and their practice (as measured in the little qualitative data and reported in the literature). Preacher training would usefully increase the self-awareness of preachers such as to close that gap.

Third, the quantitative data shows little evidence of the preachers being intentionally inductive (i.e. "poetic") in their sermon form. Hence, just as a teacher who lacks critical self-awareness may "follow their own learning styles in the way they teach" there is a risk that a preacher's preaching (i.e. teaching) style is matching their learning style and not that of the more traditional, oral, learning style of their audience. [161] Preacher training could usefully present a framework such as the Homiletic Window to ensure preachers are more intentional in varying and applying their preaching styles.

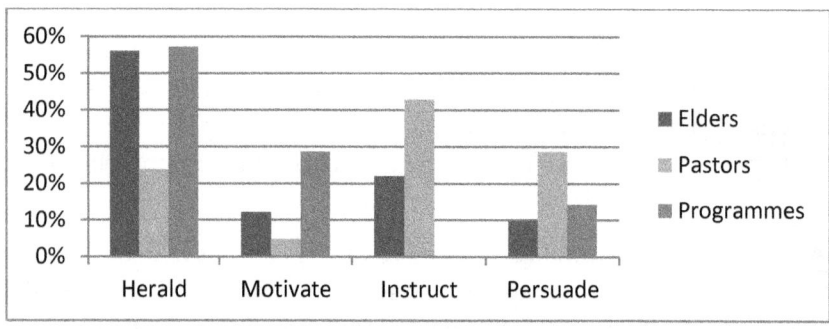

Fig. 6 – ZEC and Providers' Preaching Styles

Finally, it is informative to compare the ZEC preaching style with that (implicitly or explicitly) presented by the training programs (see Fig. 6 above). The training programs appear to match the elder's style somewhat better than the pastors because most programs seem to be dominated by classical Western thought with an emphasis on "Herald." However, while some are willing to embrace the more inductive "form" of "Motivate," none embrace "Instruct." This is important when, by analogy with learning styles, the ideal would be for the programs to be willing and able to present all legitimately "expository" preaching styles and to free preachers to embrace the oral communication models of their culture more fully. [162]

Training

Problems with "Traditional" Models

As we have already seen, both training providers and church leaders concur that preacher training is of vital importance to ZEC, and that providers view traditional training methods to be ineffective. One potentially significant difference in view, however, concerns the issue of "not training people in the right thing," with ZEC—and particularly the regional executives— not seeing it as important an issue as the training programs (see Appendix B, Fig. B24). Rightly or wrongly the college trained senior pastors do not appear to share the literature's perspective that college courses tend to be too academic. This would probably be worth considering when positioning (or "selling") the benefits of alternative training programs to potential user organisations.

Importance of Key Components

There are also some key differences in perspective between ZEC and the training program providers on the importance of the different key components of alternative training models (see Appendix B, Fig. B25). First, in aggregate ZEC interviewees appear much more supportive of home study and college integration than the training providers. This tends to align ZEC with the TEE principle that home study as critical to developing a learning culture, and the DTE interest in complimenting colleges. However, some programs clearly saw cultural difficulties with individualistic home study and a risk that college integration would devalue alternative methods.

Potential training programs and regional executives did not rate larger training conferences strongly versus smaller seminars, in line with TEE philosophy. In the case of the potential programs, this is interesting given the interview evidence that several of these programs typically rely on the conference models.

At a more detailed level, using a "least squares difference" comparison of each program's responses against the aggregate ZEC aspirations, two programs (E3 and P4) clearly showed a closer match to ZEC's perceived needs than the others.

Challenge of Leadership Culture

It was noted earlier that quantitative data from ZEC executives implied a particularly challenged leadership culture; with trust for other leaders and appreciation of the benefits of learning being particularly low (see Appendix 2, Fig. B2). Indeed, one ZEC participant affirmed: "The reason we've had problems in the church is because the leaders have never trusted each other."

This result is a useful reminder that creating the conditions for viable grassroots preacher training goes far beyond the "technical" aspects of training methods. The less tangible political and cultural issues can be just as important—if not more important—and especially when significant systemic culture change within an organisation is notoriously difficult.[163]

Profile of ZEC Needs and Provider Programs

Although my study revealed a considerable variation in individual views, some clear trends were discernible and the "Training Profile" model (see Appendix A, "Training Profile") appears to provide a particularly useful framework against which to compare training programs such as those investigated.

	Profile	Goals	Principles	CSF	Overall
E1	3	1	1	3	8
E2	3	1	1	2	7
E3	1	3	3	1	8
P1	3	2	3	2	10
P2	4	2	2	3	11
P3	2	4	4	4	14
P4	1	1	1	1	4

Fig. 7 – Fit of Programs with ZEC Needs

Discussing ZEC

A "least-squares" ranking was used to compare the self-declared profile of ZEC needs against the self-declared profile of individual training programs (see "profile" column in Fig. 7 above). This found E3 the closest match of the existing programs, and P4 the closest match of the potential programs.

However, at a more detailed level (see Appendix B, Fig. B20) none of the programs appear a particularly good match against ZEC's self-declared needs. Within the "structure" grid, most programs were insufficiently "informal" (especially E1, E2 and P2) while E3 was shown to have a "methodology" insufficiently "involved" and P1 a "structure" insufficiently "decentralised".

However, this evaluation is based on un-normalised, un-weighted analysis of self-perceptions. It might, for example, be argued that ZEC and Western run programs will have a different perspective on what "informal" means. I therefore carried out a "least-squares" ranking against my own evaluation of ZEC's needs profile. This found E1 and E2 to be the closest match of the existing programs rather than E3, while still finding P4 the closest match of the potential programs.

Goals of ZEC and Training Programs

We have seen that ZEC executives broadly saw all three of the recognised goals of "forming," "informing," and "transforming," as very important; yet my research revealed a considerable variation in declared goals among the training programs (Appendix 2, Fig. B21). For example, it is notable that E3 places a significantly lower priority on "informing" participants, as does P3 on "transforming" values and communities. Of course, this does not mean that the programs will not meet the goals that ZEC perceives as important, but it does mean that the programs are less intentional in these areas. As one program leader said: "We're less intentional about 'transforming'.... We trust in a sense that as they do the first two that it will follow."

Based on the stated goals of the training programs, a "least-squares" ranking of the data (see Fig. 7 above) found E1 and E2 as the closest match to ZEC's declared needs among the existing programs, and P4 the closest match of the potential programs.

Principles for Preacher Training

Having applied my evaluation framework to the ZEC case study, I judged the "principles" (see Appendix A, "Principles") to be the most powerful of the tools developed.

A "least-squares" ranking was used to compare the self-declared principles that ZEC needed in a program against the self-declared principles of individual training programs (see Fig. 7 above). This again found E1, E2 and E4 the closest match.

As with the "Profile" section of the evaluation, to provide a more normalised set of ratings across programs and across principles, I also rated each program based on a detailed analysis of the extensive qualitative data available. However, in general the differences between my evaluation and the self-evaluation by the program did not vary the overall "least-squares" ranking of a program, except in the case of E1 which moved from best fit (rank 1) to worst fit (rank 3) among the existing programs. I judged E1 to be significantly lower than their self-evaluation of a uniform "5" in several areas; in particular in the area of explicit multiplication.

Indeed, as with the "Profile" section, the detailed results (see Appendix B, Fig. B21) show that there is no clear outright "best fit" by any one program to the needs of ZEC. Instead, each program has relative strengths and relative weaknesses.

While these strengths and weaknesses were typically recognised by the programs, the components within the program principles section of the evaluation framework proved a valuable tool for deeper analysis.

Contextualisation of Theology

I found the potential programs to typically be driven by a centrally produced curriculum. There is little evidence of contextualisation of the theology but most said they emphasise biblical rather than systematic theology as a way of allowing students to contextualise what they heard. Some programs also had specific sessions to identify local theological issues and encourage "thinking of the Word in light of the world". Most recognised that they needed to be "more sophisticated," "targeted" and "intentional" in engaging with the context of preachers in what one program described as a cross-cultural version of the "double listening" advocated by John Stott.[164] Indeed two of the potential programs (P2 and P3) were already reviewing their curriculum to increase contextualisation. Generally, the programs recognised the challenge (identified by Strong and Strong) of addressing the theological questions of importance to the context, while "remaining committed to obeying scripture."[165] I judged it was more difficult for the more doctrinally based programs to achieve this balance (e.g. P3 which aims to be a "mini Bible college" with an emphasis on "a number of key doctrines") while those based on Bible study facilitated by local instructors (e.g. E2) was most open to context.

Contextualisation of Hermeneutics

Hermeneutics was a key focus for most of the programs, but few had addressed how "ocular" Western hermeneutic methods might be adapted for an oral sub-Saharan context. One exception to this was E2, which used a simple "memorization tool" in the local language to help oral thinkers. In its program, P4 goes further in asserting that "literacy is not superior to orality" and recognising the validity of "listening to a text" just as "it was first presented." Nevertheless, at least in principle, all programs appeared to aspire to "a biblical method for global theologizing that respects local concerns while preserving universal truth."[166]

Contextualisation of Homiletics

Few programs have explicit modules on homiletics, preferring homiletic principles to be discovered more implicitly: e.g. "Our central focus is really on the hermeneutical principles, and then the implicit work on homiletics comes out probably most in [the practical] 'do' sessions." Nevertheless, some programs present high-level homiletic principles arguing that the passage itself should "provide the shape and purpose of the sermon." The goal of avoiding presenting Western homiletic models as normative ("we are ... by no means trying to recreate American preaching in the African context") therefore results in most programs relying on supervised sermon practice to provide a more implicit training in homiletics. I would judge that—in the absence of explicit training in a contextualised homiletic—this must risk the sermon style modelled by the (often foreign) external trainers being understood as normative. Perhaps it is this risk that has resulted in one program asking itself "what does exposition look like in primarily oral, story type cultures?" with the aim of presenting a more explicit contextual homiletic within its training.

Contextualisation of Training Method

While they do not appear to have completed any formal assessment of learning styles, two of the three existing programs have considered tailoring their training method for Malawi's materially poor, oral, "field-dependent" context. One program, E2, has gone as far as saying that "if they [the students] don't have it, you [the trainer] shouldn't have it" and limit training tools to a Bible and a notebook. This program also emphasises context friendly "community based learning," where the students "discuss and articulate" using "repetition," "memorization," and a clear "story-line" to aid understanding and recall. Another existing program mixes its training methods across "preaching type" presentation, "classroom style" interactive teaching, and group discussion to "make sure people are not restricted to one type of learning." One potential program (P4) was also rated highly against this principle as it had very successfully applied a relatively sophisticated design methodology to create a tailored training method for a very similar sub-Saharan context.

Scalability

All the programs had identified the need to "train trainers" if they were to achieve the scalability required in the majority world. Some were so new (e.g. E3) that they have not gotten to that stage while others (e.g. P2) could demonstrate many examples of indigenous trainers heading "preaching movements." Some had identified the ideal of indigenous trainers being able to train trainers themselves, but some (e.g. E3) were cautious about the risks of errors beginning to creep in through this. P1 had the most intentionally integrated CPM-type multiplication techniques into its methodology.

Sustainability

Sustainability was an important principle for all the programs with, for example, an objective of P1 being the "potential for indigenous sustainability." However, there was no evidence of any program having established entirely self-sustaining movements, especially when most (at least initially) involved intercontinental flights and the time of Western trainers. In some cases, even the reproduction costs for course notes would exceed the sort of budgets identified in the ZEC survey, with one potential program quoting "something like $20 per individual per module" when running at scale. On the other hand, E2 appeared to be particularly radical in its focus, with a Bible and an empty notebook the only required participant resources, meaning a lower cost for Malawian trainers.

Bible Centric

In practice, this principle ended up denoting an "evangelical" focus on scripture as the foundation of ministry and preaching, but also the principle of concentrating on the Bible as the key textbook. On the former point, all programs were strong. On the latter point, many programs used textbooks and/or extensive notes. As discussed above, E2 was particularly aggressive on keeping material costs to a minimum. This would be a critical area for the programs to review to improve sustainability.

Practical and Skills Based

All the programs rate highly against this principle, with a primary focus on equipping trainees for practical ministry. P1 (for example) is particularly skills-oriented with a "how to" framework to the material. Others (e.g. P3) are particularly keen on practical preaching skills with every afternoon at a seminar dedicated to practising preaching.

Coaching and Discipleship

All programs referred to the importance in principle of using discipleship/coaching models to develop the practical skills of the trainees. However, many programs (e.g. P3) still appeared to operate through large seminars/conferences on approximately an annual basis with little follow-up in between, and hence mostly missed one of the essential elements of DTE/TEE principles. Nevertheless others, such as P2, encourage coaching oriented "preaching clubs" to be formed by trainees while E2 intentionally works through smaller groups and inductive discipleship techniques.

Explicit Multiplication

The programs performance against this principle mostly reflected that concerning scalability, in hindsight perhaps not surprising given how multiplication principles would drive scalability. Once again, P1 demonstrated the most intentional focus on rapid multiplication techniques with their model expecting people who have been trained to quickly go on to create a "2nd generation" of trained preachers and hence achieve "breadth through a ... multiplication strategy." At the other end of the spectrum, the program framework for E1 precludes local trainers from training trainers because of the perceived risk of doctrinal error creeping in.

Critical Success Factors

In Chapter 2, I highlighted that the "Principles" section and the CSF section of the evaluation framework used in my study were derived from different knowledge domains which came to similar conclusions about what might contribute to effective grassroots preacher training. It should therefore not be surprising that the results from the CSF framework duplicated somewhat those from the Principles framework. Nevertheless, the detailed quantitative and qualitative responses by the interviewees provide some additional useful insights.

One such insight is that "empowering trainers to innovate" might be a critical factor to ensure contextualisation but it is not practised in a significant way by the potential programs. This may show nervousness by some about losing control of contextualising through partnership. Another example is "ensuring integration into the overall strategy of the local church" which appeared to be recognised by all as desirable if common ground was to be achieved. However, some programs have found it challenging to find such common ground, e.g. African partner churches "all say they want leadership courses ... [b]ut very few ever ask for courses that actually teach them how to preach the Bible properly."

While some programs (especially P1 and P4) recognise the difficulty of keeping things "simple, low-cost, and reproducible," most do not appear as intentional about this. I would judge the relatively high self-assessment of most programs to be too optimistic. This probably indicates that the magnitude of the challenge to achieve real sustainability has not been entirely understood. Potentially, E2 and P4 are showing a more radical approach that deserves more attention—where the Bible and an empty notebook are combined with coaching/discipleship and reflective practices for the maximum opportunity for scalability and sustainability.

Summary Overview of Training Program

In comparing the programs, either qualitatively or quantitatively, it is critical to recognise the focus of each program. For example, the focus of E2 and E3 is primarily on discipleship training and general leadership, while the other programs focus more specifically on a mix of hermeneutics and preaching.

In addition, the qualitative results (see Appendix B, Fig. B16 for a summary) have repeatedly demonstrated the distinct strengths and weaknesses of the individual programs. This is also reflected quantitatively (Fig. 7 above) in the way different programs vary in "least-squares" rank against ZEC needs for different aspects of the evaluation framework.

We must recognise that the conclusions from this quantitative analysis are highly provisional and of necessity are based on self-evaluation by the training program rather than direct evaluation of the programs in action. Nevertheless, bearing in mind the top-level qualitative summary of program weaknesses identified in Appendix B, Fig. B16, the following broad evaluation can be made for the case study context of ZEC in Malawi. First, the existing programs had—across all aspects of the evaluation framework—a very similar degree of match to ZEC's needs, but with E2 appearing slightly the better match due to it being specifically designed for Malawi, highly contextualised, and with proven scalability (with the Bible as its only textbook). Second, among the potential programs, P4 appears the best match. Again, this is due to this program being highly contextualised, and designed in Africa for Africa by a team who truly understand local learning styles.

Chapter 5: Doing Better

Conclusions

The primary question which I had investigated in my study was: *What does the example of the Zambezi Evangelical Church in Malawi tell us about the viability of training grassroots preachers in sub-Saharan Africa in a way that is contextual, scalable and sustainable?*

I have set out the main conclusions of my study point by point below:

Context

Conclusion: The ministerial context of Zambezi Evangelical Church in Malawi is an especially challenging one.

This fundamental premise of the study is supported by the evidence from the case study. The country is economically very poor and faces significant spiritual challenges. In turn, ZEC is challenged economically and hindered by widespread nominalism and syncretism. Despite many strengths and opportunities, ZEC in Malawi makes for an especially good test environment within which to evaluate the viability of alternative grassroots preacher training methods.

Preaching

The literature and primary research also justifies several conclusions concerning preaching in Malawi. In general, there was no indication that these findings would not be valid more widely within sub-Saharan Africa.

Conclusion: Preaching is of particular importance in the rural sub-Saharan context.

The primary research strongly validates the assertion in the literature of the priority of preaching and its pragmatic importance in an oral culture context where it is the only way many hear the Word.

Conclusion: The wide range of problems identified in the literature concerning grassroots preaching in rural sub-Saharan Africa is valid.

Although many pastors have received training, my study has shown that untrained preachers are doing most of the preaching in ZEC, to relatively large congregations, and with little preparation or grounding in the Word.

Conclusion: ZEC affirms, in principle, the expository foundations of preaching.

This is likely a factor of the ZEC heritage rather than typical of sub-Saharan Africa. However, it is important to recognise this point if appropriately contextualised training is to be achieved.

Conclusion: ZEC preachers exhibit all the preaching styles of the Homiletic Window.

However, perhaps surprisingly, elders show the stereotypically Western style of "Herald". Further research is warranted on this topic, but it can certainly be argued that contextualised preacher training needs to present and enable the full spectrum of preaching styles.

Learning

The rich qualitative and quantitative results of the research allow tentative conclusions concerning learning in Malawi that are consistent with at least one other sub-Saharan region.

Conclusion: ZEC preachers predominantly exhibit the learning style preferences of "Reflector" and "Theorist".

The consensus in the literature that sub-Saharan Africans are generally "field dependent" learners was not directly tested but is consistent with the empirical results. More importantly, the results showing a range of LSQ learning styles clearly indicate that training programs need to intentionally consider learning styles in their design/delivery, but also need to be flexible in assessing the needs of individual learners and different groups as much as perceived cultural norms.

Preacher Training

We can now move to the primary focus of this study, and draw conclusions concerning grassroots preacher training within the context.

Conclusion: Grassroots ZEC pastors and ZEC executives alike give preacher training a high priority.

Clearly, the lack of preacher training is not because it is seen as fundamentally unimportant by the user constituent.

Conclusion: Training providers affirm the foundational importance of expository preaching.

This is hardly a surprising conclusion given the doctrinal heritage of the training providers evaluated. Nevertheless, it shows an important and critical theological alignment between them and ZEC.

Conclusion: Traditional training models are incapable of adequately meeting the needs of rural sub-Saharan Africa.

While recognising their value in developing pastors and church leaders, ZEC and the training providers validate the literature in acknowledging the limitations of Bible colleges in reaching grassroots preachers.

Conclusion: The preacher training curriculum must not ignore personal spiritual development.

At all levels of ZEC, the perceived need is for preacher training to encompass personal spiritual development as well as a broad range of "technical" subjects. An especially narrow focus on homiletics would not suffice.

Conclusion: Within limits, contextualisation of theology, hermeneutics, homiletics, and training method are all vitally important for the effectiveness of preacher training in sub-Saharan Africa.

The underlying presupposition of my study and the literature that such contextualisation is important appears to have been validated by all parties through their responses. Indirect validation also comes from the fact that programs such as P2 and P3 see shortfalls in this area as worthy of a major program review.

Finally, and most importantly,

Conclusion: The example of Zambezi Evangelical Church in Malawi tell us that the contextual, scalable and sustainable training of grassroots preachers in sub-Saharan Africa is certainly feasible but challenging to make fully viable.

My study appears to show that effective preacher training (i.e. that is contextual, scalable and sustainable) is *feasible* (i.e. it is in theory possible) in the sense that each of the derived principles and critical success factors explored are present to some extent in ZEC and in at least one of the programs. However, the research also suggests that it is very challenging for such training to be truly *viable* (i.e. practically achievable in reality) in this (and similar) contexts because ZEC does not adequately demonstrate the necessary conditions for success, and no single training program exhibits all the derived principles and necessary success factors. This may go part of the way to explain why TEE has struggled to fully achieve the promises claimed for it in its early years.

Briefly summarising each aspect:

1. *ZEC Leadership Culture:* This needs urgent attention, and change, if any training is to be successful, and in particular alternative coaching oriented models. It needs to be recognised that implementing this scale of cultural change is not trivial. Low mutual trust will be particularly challenging.
2. *ZEC Strategic Planning:* A more robust approach to strategic planning is required within ZEC. Preacher training requires a strategy that fits within a broader training strategy which sits within a larger organisational strategy.
3. *Contextual theology:* More needs to be done to ensure the training programs address the contextually relevant theological challenges expressed by the preachers. While most training programs have abandoned a doctrine-driven approach for a more contextually flexible approach of applying principles of Bible interpretation to

the context, it is only the minority of programs (e.g. P1 and E1) that have so far worked this fully into their program.

4. *Contextual hermeneutics:* This is a particular priority. There needs to be a wider implementation of a more contextualised hermeneutic by the training programs, and more explicit and intentional training in this hermeneutic. Few have adopted methodologies explicitly designed for majority world oral cultures. The use of Richard's "Scripture Sculpture" by P4 is a positive move but more could be done to build on the explicitly oral techniques developed by Chifungo.[167]

5. *Contextual Homiletics:* More emphasis is needed within the programs on specifically and intentionally training contextually appropriate homiletic skills. Any concerns about fostering Western preaching models can and should be ameliorated by clearly explaining the value of suitably "sanctified" oral communication techniques—with or without reference to the frameowrk provided by the Homiletic Window model. Grassroots pastors could then be intentionaly "given permission" to use these techniques while being faithful to the foundational principles of expository preaching.

6. *Contextual methods:* Most programs appear to give consideration to contextualisation of the training methods. However, none of the programs seem to have fully implemented and sustained all four components of DTE. Particularly important for improved viability is an increased emphasis on enabling highly localised coaching (perhaps using equiped and empowered pastors) within regular small group seminars (the "Preachers' Clubs" of P2).

7. *Scalability:* Some programs, e.g. P1, have implemented this relatively well. However, few have demonstrated intentional multiplication to realise multi-generational "self-propagating" movements. More work needs to be done to evaluate the right balance of multiplication versus 'quality control' of the training being provided.

8. *Sustainability:* This is perhaps the greatest challenge of all. None of the programs evaluated appear to have become "self-supporting" and most do not seem to recognise the full challenge of doing so in a context where perhaps only £1.50 per student per month is

available. Learning from E2 and P4, more radical approaches appear to be required where core resources are limited to the Bible, an empty notebook, and simple key reflective practices taught orally in small local groups.

Framework, Methods and Tools

Conclusion: The field work provisionally demonstrates considerable merit in the analytical framework, methods, and tools as an approach to evaluating alternatives for preacher training in sub-Saharan Africa.

Although admittedly limited to a particular context (ZEC, Malawi), in general the framework under discussion was well received by user and provider communities alike: e.g. "This [framework] will benefit many." At the very least, the final quantitative ranking of programs against ZEC's needs did not appear unreasonable.

Of particular note was the value of the "Leadership Culture" model in determining how strategically prepared a user organisation is to effectively collaborate with a training provider. However, it was the "Principles" section that in practice proved the most powerful component of the evaluation framework.

The use of extensive triangulation between qualitative and quantitative data added depth to the analysis and helped identify suspected "researcher effect" and "prestige bias". However, this methodology produces large amounts of qualitative data and a workload that future researchers should be prepared for.

Generally, the specific questionnaire tools used proved effective. However, the difficulty preachers had interpreting the "semantic differential scale" questions would suggest that, in future, they should be reformatted as "matrix questions."

Recommendations

While the type of grassroots preacher training envisaged may not be demonstrably viable, nevertheless each program has shown particular strengths, and some appear a better match to ZEC's present needs. This allows some clear recommendations to be made, which could be seen as moving towards a practical theology for training grassroots preachers in sub-Saharan Africa.

Providers

What recommendations, if any, can be derived from the case study for *Providers of preacher training in rural sub-Saharan Africa*?

1. Create stronger forums for the sharing of experience and expertise between programs. This could lead to greater differentiation and more complimentary offerings. It would also allow greater sharing of best practice in different elements of preacher training discovered in this study.
2. Ensure more components of the DTE model are established within the programs, in particular frequent (e.g. monthly) small-scale, "preaching clubs" that would encourage ongoing coaching between less-frequent symposiums.
3. Accelerate existing reviews, or start reviews, concerning the contextualisation of the theology, and radically review the hermeneutic models being used in oral cultures such as sub-Saharan Africa.
4. Maintain the modelling of good homiletics, but consider enhancing the explicit training on homiletics. Use broad frameworks such as the Homiletic Window where appropriate but, regardless, ensure programs appropriately validate and promote oral/inductive communication styles. The use of an explicit homiletic framework will allow inductive and deductive forms to be encouraged while correcting the worst excesses of both.
5. Challenge the viability of existing training methods to enable real scalability ("self-propagation") and sustainability ("self-sustaining") and seriously evaluate more radical models to

establish training movements with significantly reduced unit training costs.

ZEC

What recommendations, if any, can be derived from the case study for *ZEC in rural Malawi?*

1. Courageously address the significant issues with ZEC leadership culture. In particular, to develop greater trust among leaders and openness to discussing training needs.
2. Invest in greater clarity of overall organisational strategy and top-level training strategy. Clearly position preacher training within this strategic framework, and use it to evaluate the success of any launched program.
3. Do not re-invent the wheel. Establish a long-term exclusive strategic partnership with one or two existing preacher training programs to integrate the best of the existing programs and tailor them for ZEC needs. Decisions on such strategic relationships should be driven by a broad range of factors and the alignment of strategic objectives and the ability to form close working partnerships. However, the results of this study would suggest ZEC might first consider E2 as partners for their general discipleship/leadership program while selecting a program such as P4 or P2 to build a more specialist preaching course.
4. Be sure to integrate fully the preacher training program into the existing leadership structure, with the Kotale as the main organisational hub.
5. Integrate suitable existing pastors into the program as coach/trainers to maximise use of existing skills and minimise resistance to change.
6. Strategically coordinate with the Evangelical Bible College of Malawi (EBCoM) so every newly graduated ZEC pastor understands what ZEC expects of them as leader/coach, and so they emerge fully trained as coaches for the selected preacher training program.

7   Investigate the feasibility of preachers being selected by the pastor from the available church elders on the basis of passion, gifting, and skills, rather than all church elders being expected to preach.

Wider Church in Malawi and Sub-Saharan Africa

What recommendations, if any, can be derived from the case study for *Churches in search of preacher training in rural sub-Saharan Africa?*

1   Consider using the evaluation framework established through this research to develop a clear strategic framework for grassroots preacher training in their context.

2   Don't reinvent the wheel. Evaluate the profiles of the various training programs presented within this study and consider strategic reuse.

3   There is a clear need to investigate the opportunity for greater coordination across user organisations concerning requirements for grassroots preacher training across Malawi churches. This might be facilitated through the Evangelical Alliance of Malawi and possibly more widely through the Association for Christian Theological Education in Africa (ACTEA).

Further Work

This work suggests several areas worthy of further investigation. These include the following.

1   *Preaching styles:* There would be value in extending the research on preaching styles to other churches in Malawi to validate the conclusion that contextualised preacher training needs to enable all preaching styles of the Homiletic Window. A comparison of results between Malawi and UK samples could usefully illuminate any cultural dependencies.

2   *Learning styles*: Further work comparing UK and Malawi preachers, and comparing preachers with other professional groups could usefully contribute to the debate on the relative importance of culture and profession in determining learning styles.

3   *Analytical framework*: The framework would benefit from evaluation and use in a wider range of contexts including other churches in Malawi and other parts of sub-Saharan Africa.

4   *Analytical framework*: A larger sample of results would allow factor analysis to de-duplicate/normalise similar elements of the "Principles" and "Critical Success Factors" models to create a single more coherent model of primary "Principles" (e.g. "Scalability") and secondary "Features" (e.g. "explicit multiplication.")

5   *Homiletic Window*: As with my prior work in the UK, the Homiletic Window appeared to show value as an aid for conceptualising key aspects of the homiletic.[168] However, this instrument needs further use across several researchers and a wider sample size to check "test-retest" reliability, "inter-rater" reliability and "instrument" validity. Multi-variance testing of specific questions could also be used to tune the instrument.

6   *Learning Styles Questionnaire:* The Honey & Mumford framework would benefit from further simplification of the English and Chichewa versions to enable it to gain wider acceptance.

So, the most recent phase of my journey of discovery concerning the potential of grassroots preacher training in sub-Saharan Africa is complete.

Academically, the power of the practical theology method allowed insights to be deployed from diverse knowledge domains. It also verified the need for, and desire for, preacher training within ZEC and outlined the significant opportunity of alternative training models in meeting that need. The extensive qualitative and quantitative results indicate the feasibility of such alternative models, and structured analysis has allowed critical recommendations to be made to both user and provider organisations that move us towards a practical theology for viable and effective grassroots preacher training in sub-Saharan Africa, and indeed appears to validate Bowers' perspective concerning African theological education that "in this day, in this hour, on this continent, there is really no higher calling."[169]

Theologically, the New Testament endorsed training model of coaching/discipleship (so famously captured in 2 Tim 2:2) still appears uniquely relevant to the low-resource, oral and relational context that rural Africa finds itself in.

Personally, the study has facilitated a most productive introduction to my new ministerial context, while creating an unexpectedly rich foundation for the next stage in my ministry in the "warm heart of Africa;" serving local preachers as they master their craft. For, as Davis expressed so aptly, whether it is in the wealthy cities of Europe or the dusty villages of Malawi:

> *A man determined to preach his best has before him, like any artist, a lifelong struggle with form.*[170]

Chapter 6: Preach the Word

My original field research for this study was carried out in early 2015. Since then there have been several developments of note.

ZEC

The first major development came in late 2015 as the ZEC leadership demonstrated significant courage in completing an open, Bible driven, strategic review. This included a meaningful discussion about the major cultural issues identified in my study; especially the lack of trust within ZEC, and the low priority given to training.

The resulting strategic plan presented a renewed task for ZEC to be "Discipling Nations for Christ," while for the first time establishing explicit organisational values including those of "integrity" and "openness" which intentionally address the issue of trust.

While it is too early to evaluate the impact of this move, ZEC leadership are beginning to engage with my first recommendation that they address the significant issues with ZEC leadership culture (in particular the lack of trust), and my second recommendation that they invest in creating a clear, overall organisational strategy. Already there is clear evidence—not least within key governance forums—that this is bringing early benefits.

ZEC's review also identified two key strategic priorities for the church: biblical leadership (to select, develop and support leaders who demonstrate Christ-like, transformational, servant leadership) and biblical discipleship (to make, nurture, and grow mature disciples of Christ who are in turn enabled to make disciples). Their resulting portfolio of strategic initiatives covers objectives as diverse as the more rigorous development of church doctrine, through to strengthening of children's ministry, and the re-envisioning of the church's historic operation of health centres and hospitals. However, given the low priority given to training within ZEC in the past, they importantly recognised the need for a robust set of complimentary denomination-wide training programs if they were to fully address the two key strategic priorities.

ZEC Training

Within this overall strategic framework, a motivated team of ZEC leaders worked with the denomination's General Secretary and his deputy to develop a set of training programs addressing their two strategic priorities of discipleship and leadership development. Having defined their needs, they followed my third recommendation to avoid re-inventing the wheel, and rapidly implemented their training strategy using two existing relationships.

Discipleship Training

ZEC engaged with Disciple the Nations (DtN) to implement training geared at discipling church members and equipping church members to disciple others.

DtN is a small, well-established Malawi based mission specialising in practical theological training. They were natural partners, as DtN's cross-denominational training events had already benefited ZEC for many years; their senior staff are ZEC pastors who are also trained educationalists and experienced curriculum developers, and there has been a close partnership for many years.

This resulted in the rapid re-launch of an existing discipleship program and annual discipleship conference targeted more specifically at ZEC needs, including a program giving practical guidance on sexual morality to youth.

Leadership Training

ZEC also engaged with J-Life Ministries in Malawi to implement a general, Bible-based program focused on discipling and equipping for church leaders.

Like DtN, J-Life Ministries is also well-established. It is involved in discipling youth, training church leaders, and providing relief aid. It is led by a senior leader of ZEC and most senior staff are ZEC pastors or elders.

This close relationship with ZEC allowed the rapid re-launch of an existing cross-denominational program called Learn2Serve, but now targeted more specifically at ZEC leaders across Malawi. Learn2Serve itself was developed and is operated as a partnership between J-Life Ministries and Kerusso Trust in the UK. The program consists of four one-week modules aimed at discipling rural church leaders and training them in biblical leadership and practical ministry.

DtN also worked with the ZEC leadership to develop a Pastors' Seminar and an Elders' Conference that were launched in 2017 and are being rolled out across the country in five regional locations. These events focus specifically on communicating the ZEC strategy, understanding the biblical role of pastors and elders, and providing practical tools to support those roles.

Preach the Word

Within this wider training portfolio, ZEC gave significant priority to the development of a new grassroots preacher training program. And, with their renewed strategic plan and the new leadership training strategy, ZEC was—in line with my second recommendation—able to clearly position preacher training within a strong wider strategic framework.

From the outset, the leadership also addressed my fourth recommendation, and decided to use the Kotale as the main route to organising the preacher training events. Indeed, the strategic objective set for the program is that by 2021 every preacher in ZEC will have had the opportunity to complete a preacher training course within their local Kotale district.

Program development

In the meantime, during Malawi's 2015 dry season, I had the opportunity to pilot some of the ideas emerging from this study in the form of four sessions of preaching training within a week-long cross-denominational Pastors Bookset Conference run by Zambesi Mission (my parent organisation and historically the main mission partner to ZEC). The very positive response from the pastors encouraged me to further develop and pilot a two-day ZEC preacher training event in five district centres in the north of Malawi during the 2016 dry season.

Based on the positive results from that pilot, the ZEC leadership commissioned me to develop a more robust program for national deployment within ZEC. I did this in partnership with DtN, so as to gain from their curriculum development expertise, deep contextual expertise, experience of working with ZEC at the local level, and their passion to continue operating the program in partnership with ZEC after my Malawi deployment finished in late 2017.

Overview

Called "Preach the Word" (PtW), the new three module training program (see Fig. 8) started rolling out in May 2017. It carefully targets the needs and capabilities of ZEC's grassroots preachers as they were identified in my study. ZEC and DtN leadership agreed a clear need for practical, contextual, scalable, and sustainable preacher training that can be delivered to the preachers right where they are, with a target audience of men and women with some experience of preaching but limited preacher training and limited formal education. Their vision is to create in this way a vibrant community of trained preachers better able to expound Scripture.

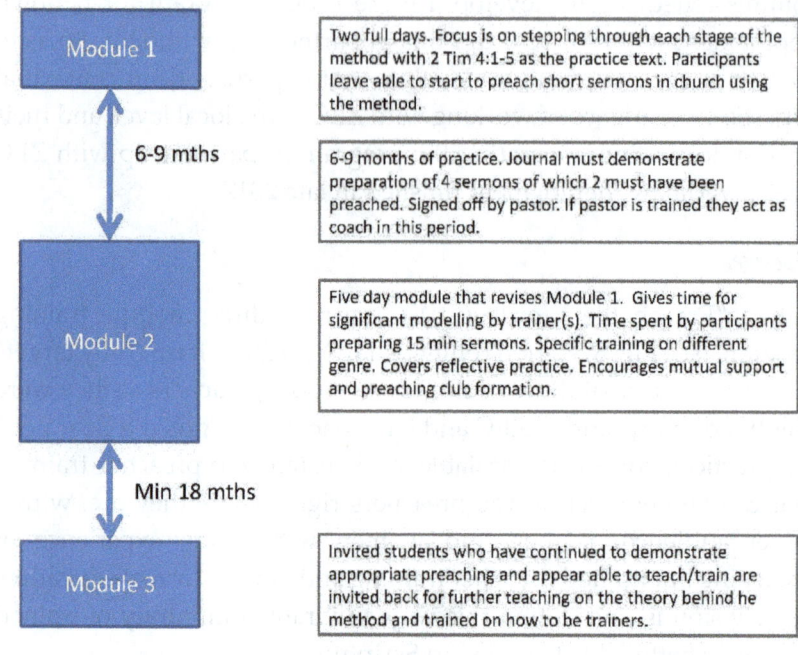

Fig. 8 Overview of the Three-module Program

The program is tightly focussed on the practice of preaching, avoids doctrinally-based training, and intentionally relies on other programs in the portfolio—such as the Learn2Serve partnership between J-Life Ministries and The Kerusso Trust—to develop the broader Bible appreciation needed for truly effective preaching.

The overall program follows key high-level design principles established from my study; aiming to obtain a high degree of contextualisation, scalability and sustainability using a wide range of elements from Diversified Theological Education (DTE). For more detail see the example session plans for Module 1 provided in Appendix C.

For example, the curriculum has been kept simple and tightly structured to aid scalability by simplifying the task of training new trainers. Two DtN coaches (who are also ZEC pastors) have already been trained, starting as my interpreters in early training events and carrying out the critical task of translating course material into Chichewa. They are now facilitating Module 1 training themselves in Chichewa.

Learning from E2 and P2, the program supports sustainability by using minimal materials. Participants are encouraged to take notes in their own words in a low-cost school notebook, and the optional brief course notes available at the end of the module are locally copied at a cost of less than £0.50 which is charged on to participants to ensure they value the notes.

Similarly, the requirements made by the program on the local facilities are also kept low. The trainers restrict themselves to a regular flipchart pad which is carried to the event on low-cost public transport and clamped to an upturned bench or table that acts as an easel. The training schedule is limited to daylight hours so no electricity is required, and the facilitators eat and sleep with the participants to minimise cost and administration.

The district Kotale is also responsible for managing and funding the venue for the event (usually a church building) and accomodation/subsistance for the participants. This ensures the program is appropriately resourced and priced for the context.

Module 1: We Preach the Word

The first module of the program is intentionally limited at 2 days to encourage maximum participation from rural preachers. The aim is to have 35–50 participants to make effective use of the trainers' time while still ensuring an interactive seminar-type atmosphere.

After a model sermon from one of the trainers, the first module develops the ideas of Jem Hovil and BUILD Partners, and helps participants explore the importance of preaching, the character/calling of the preacher, and key Biblical principles of preaching (see Appendix C, "Module 1 – Session 1.")[171]

Right from this first session, the program also allows for both cultural and individual learning preferences. For example, small-group studies on Bible texts and homiletic questions are used to encourage reflection and inductive reasoning from Scripture, "grounded" practical examples are used throughout the program, participants are encouraged to think things through to the stage of concrete action plans, and there are summary periods of propositional presentation by the trainer. While this approach requires careful facilitation by a theologically and contextually mature trainer, it also allows for the maximum contextualisation of the theological content by that training.

In Session 2 (see Appendix C, "Overview of Module 1") participants are then introduced to one particular hermeneutic/homiletic method that helps the preacher match the theological principles of preaching that they have discovered. Again, following the example of BUILD Partners, I used a much-simplified adaptation of the "Scripture Sculpture" method of Richard.[172] Fig. 9 shows the high-level view of my simplified version based on Module 1, Unit 13 of Jem Hovil's curriculum.[173] It became "Sculpting Sermons with Scripture" in the simplified English of the PtW program as this was found to be more understandable by English speaking Malawians.

I consider "Sculpture Sermons with Scripture" to be particularly appropriate for the oral culture of Malawi, especially because of its very memorable, visual, and concrete core metaphor. Also, it usefully uses one framework to cover both the hermeneutic stage and the homiletic stage of sermon preparation, and is flexible enough to allow for significant contextualisation of both stages.

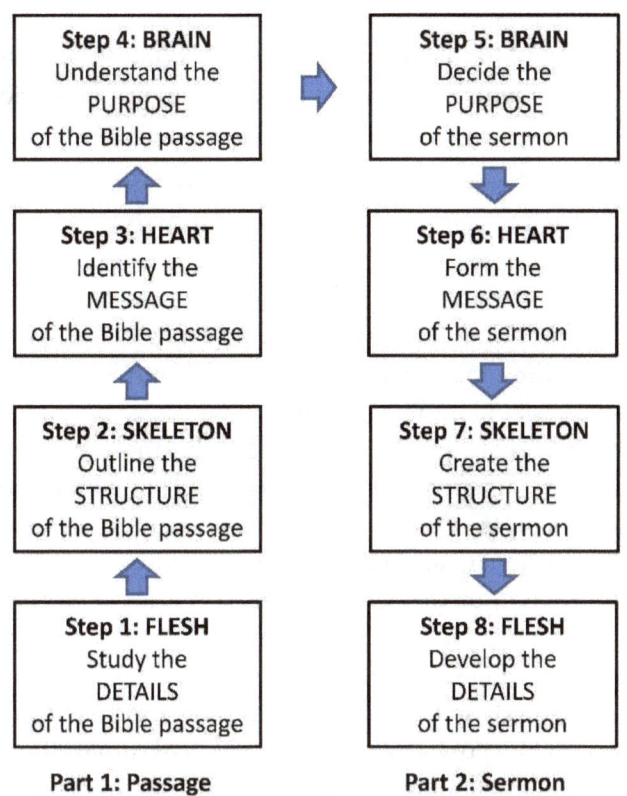

Fig. 9 – Sculpting Sermons with Scripture

Part 1 of Sculpting Sermons with Scripture is the hermeneutic stage of the method. The program contextualises this part of the method in a similar way to that proposed by Chifungo.[174] Hence, the program explicitly recognises and allows for the fact that competent preachers can be functionally illiterate and be listening to a Scripture passage rather than reading it. While emphasising key universal hermeneutic principles, the program also encouraged the Malawian preacher to exploit the fact that their oral, community rich, respect-focussed, subsistence-oriented village culture is close to the culture of the Bible, and then to imaginatively use that implicit understanding of Bible culture as they seek to understand the original meaning of the text. These points are emphasised, illustrated, and demonstrated throughout Sessions 2–6 as they cover Step 1–Step 4 of the method, but are specifically covered in Session 8, "Understanding Orality" (see

Appendix C, "Overview of Module 1.") The first day also includes (see Appendix C, "Module 1 – Session 5") a more didactic session helping the participants to discover the specific characteristics of a Bible letter.

Part 2 of Sculpting Sermons with Scripture is the homiletic stage of the method. The program contextualises this part of the method following the principles of the Homiletic Window. Using simple terms and practical demonstrations, preachers are shown how to "exegete" the needs and context of today's Malawian congregations as they consider how the original message and purpose of the Bible text might be translated into their sermon's message and purpose for today's listeners. This approach ensures a balanced view of the Pastor/Proclaimer function of the sermon. The curiculum also explains in simple terms the difference between the deductive/propositional approach of the Philosopher and the inductive/narrative approach of the Poet to the form of a sermon. Participants are then encouraged to intentionally study and embrace the oral communication skills of their culture and to use them, while keeping those methods subservient to the objective of communicating the message and purpose of the text. So, for example, the use of illustration, narrative, and cultural rhetorical techniques are encouraged, but the preacher is also encouraged to use Bible stories and proverbs to illustrate a sermon rather than a traditional story with a suspect moral. Again, all this is emphasised, illustrated, and demonstrated in Sessions 7–12 but is specifically covered in Session 8, "Understanding Orality" (see Appendix C, "Overview of Module 1.")

Participants are carefully coached in each of the eight steps of Sculpting Sermons with Scripture with each step being practiced on the module's key text: 2 Timothy 4:1–5. At each step the small groups present their findings back to the seminar as a whole, creating significant opportunities for further learning and coaching. In addition, in Session 6 and Session 11 (as time permits) the participants practice applying the whole of Part 1 and Part 2 respectively on the fresh passage of Titus 1:5–9.

Module 1 intentionally focuses on preaching from "ideas driven" Bible writing, and in particular the Epistles. This genre typically presents the original author's message and purpose in the clearest way, and hence simplifies the task for the participants as they (often for the first time) practice structured exegesis and sermon planning. The module also intentionally uses two passages that cover the topic of preaching and the character of a church leader. In this way, as the participants practice the method the class also discovers key biblical principles for their role as preachers and leaders.

In the Malawi context it is normal—and has been found to be extremely helpful—to encourage consistent attendance at all sessions in the module through the formal awarding of an attendance certificate at the end of the seminar.

Preaching Journal

At least 6 months is expected to elapses between Module 1 and 2 during which the participants are required to keep a journal of their preaching, recording how they applied Sculpting Sermons with Scripture as they prepared their sermon. At least four examples are expected to be presented in the journal, with at least two having been actually preached. The journal is signed-off by the student's Pastor prior to Module 2. This stage is intended to encourage ongoing practice of what has been learned in the participants real day-to-day context, and to test their commitment prior to Module 2. DtN facilitators follow up once or twice with individuals by phone during this period to encourage them. However, the practice of reflective writing is not a cultural norm and we are monitoring this stage of the program carefully.

ZEC pastors are fully integrated into the program and expected to attend the course with their church elders. Many have experienced little or no preacher training since their time at Bible college and recognise the benefit they gain from attending, but we also emphasise their need to fill an ongoing role as coaches to their local preachers. This helps surmount the cultural barrier to a leader such as a pastor admitting they need training. A church Pastor and their local elders are also encouraged to form local "preacher groups" to facilitate this ongoing revision and practice, with the wider aim of instututionalising a cultural change within ZEC.

Module 2: We Preach the Whole Word

At the time of writing, the pilot curriculum for Module 2 is about to be used for the first time. This module lasts for five days as it is expected that participants who have satisfactoraly attended Module 1 and completed a preaching journal will be sufficiently motivated to attend the longer seminar. The longer time available, with what is expected to be a smaller group of students, allows for extensive modelling of expository preaching by the trainers, and for attendees to present short sermons to the seminar.

This module intentionally follows the approach of P2 and structures the day (see Appendix C, "Overview of Module 2") into an early morning session, investigating the specific characteristics of a Bible genre, while the rest of the day is spent with participants in small groups applying Sculpting Sermons with Scripture to an example text from that genre.

The seminar starts with significant time spent revising Module 1, and also encouraging discussion by the participants about their experience of applying the method between Module 1 and 2. However, the main focus of the module is on the application of the method to a wider set of Bible genres: specifically narrative, poetry, and parables. Narrative is particularly important in the Malawi context where the oral culture attracts preachers to Bible stories and there is a propensity to use story within the sermon. Poetry and parables are contextually important as genres which are readily misinterpreted by the undertrained preacher. The complexities of preaching from prophecy meant it could not be included in this module.

Module 3

Following principles established by DtN in other programs, Preach the Word will monitor the performance of attendees and follow the progress of key individuals (especially pastors) after their satisfactory completion of Module 2. Attendees who continue to demonstrate effective application of the principles and method, and who are judged both able to teach and teachable, will be invited back for further training. This will revise the material in Module 1 and 2, explain more of the theology and principles underlying the method, and coach the individuals in the program's approach to training. Successful participants will then be ready to start work as apprentice course facilitators or be recognised as fully trained local preaching coaches.

It is too early to judge results, but my expectation is that involving pastors in the program from Module 1, encouraging them to form preacher groups at their local church and monitor the participants' journals, and in particular using Module 3 to train pastors as trainers will all help to (as I suggested in my fifth recommendation) minimise resistance to change from the pastors.

College integration

By design, Preach the Word also aims to follow my sixth recommendation (and the lessons from Diversified Theologial Education) and ensure close coordination with the Evangelical Bible College of Malawi (EBCoM).

ZM and ZEC are founder members of EBCoM and most ZEC pastors are trained there. In 2016 I was invited to teach preaching to the students following the English language undergraduate diploma course at the college. With the full support of ZEC and EBCoM, I used the oportunity to develop a more academic, semester long version of Preach the Word that ensured students left the college with a full appreciation of the preaching methodology being taught to preachers within ZEC. The practical and structured approach of the diploma course was well received by the college and the students. There are also plans in academic year 2017/18 to offer Module 1 and Module 2 of Preach the Word as an optional activity for all students.

In this way it is hoped that every newly graduated ZEC pastor understands what ZEC expects of them as a preacher, and that they emerge fully trained as coaches for Preach the Word in their churches.

Looking Forward

It is too early to make any full and firm conclusions about how effectively PtW integrates the recommendations of my initial study, or how well it meets the needs of ZEC. While Module 1 is now fully operational in Chichewa within ZEC, Module 2 has just started its initial roll-out. However, there are already distinct encouragements and challenges.

Early experience has emphasised how critical it is that preacher-focussed training like PtW sits within a broader leadership training program such as that of ZEC. No matter how effective the hermeneutic/homiletic model, on its own it cannot make up for the very low level of Bible understanding demonstrated by many grassroots preachers in the early roll-out of Preach the Word. However slow it might appear to western eyes, it is profoundly encouraging that the deep spiritual culture change being attempted by ZEC is being powered by a training portfolio that helps its preachers broaden their underlying Bible knowledge, and deepen their personal spiritual maturity, as well as practice practical preaching skills.

Of special encouragement has been the enthusiastic reaction of the preachers to the fact that the program embraces orality within its hermeneutic/homiletic model. In the trusting environment of the contextually-aware small-group training model there have been many instances where functionally-illiterate rural preachers have demonstrated the effectiveness of the method when they are restricted to listening at home to a family member read the Bible to them.

Early results have also been encouraging in terms of the dedication and enthusiasm of those who attend the training course, and the way those trained are beginning to champion the program and its methods within the denomination through word of mouth. However, there are several challenges that the program is still adapting to. For example, while the ZEC Kotale remains the natural coordination point for the program, it has been very evident that—in Patterson's words—we are providing "pastoral education on a poverty level."[175] Even within such a relatively small geographic area, the cost of transport often appears to hinder involvement by grassroots preachers. And the relatively low attendance of male church elders is at least in part down to the challenges the "bread winner" faces in being released from daily work. This is exacerbated by the relatively poor time, resource management, and forward planning skills of many grassroots leaders, which often leads to the disapointment of last minute schedule changes.

It certainly remains clear that in the sub-Saharan context, flexibility by the training organisation—both tactically and strategically—remains critically important. It is therefore of the greatest encouragement that DtN demonstrates a clear commitment to this sort of flexibility and continuous improvement.

So, while the jury is out, a couragious journey of Bible-based culture change has certainly been initiated by ZEC; one that parallels my personal life-changing journey described in the introduction, which for me started in 2013 when I picked up Kinsler's *"Ministry by the People."*[176] My hope in writing this book is that my journey will in some way help yours; whether it is in encouraging you to apply the broad principals of Practical Theology to your real world ministry challenges, to strive for more effective training of grassroots leaders in majority world churches, or to recognise that in the post-occular and post-Christendom West we have a lot to learn from the oral communication methods and alternative training models of our African brothers.

However, if nothing else, this Malawian journey has re-emphasised for me that God's chosen approach to saving this world from its seemingly overwhelming and systemic, material and spiritual, problems remains as it ever has been: to save the world one human heart at a time. And today, as it ever has been, the expository preaching of God's word remains a primary tool within the work of the Holy Sprit to bring about that heart change. For, if everyone who calls on the name of the Lord will be saved ...

How, then, can they call on the one they have not believed in? And how can they believe in the one of whom they have not heard? And how can they hear without someone preaching to them? (Romans 10:14)

Appendix A – Quantitative Evaluation Framework

Here I summarise the quantitative framework that was developed in Chapter 1 to evaluate the effectiveness of grassroots preacher training, including examples of the question formats described in Chapter 2. I hope this might help researchers to reuse the evaluation framework within another context. My dissertation provides more information on the qualitative framework used, as well as specific details on how the qualitative and quantitative aspects of the framework were applied to different user and provider communities.[1]

ZEC Leadership Culture

This particularly sensitive section of the evaluation framework was only used as part of the guided-questionnaire with ZEC denominational leaders at regional and national level to evaluate the user organisation's leadership culture.

(For the following questions tick the box that best describes your level of agreement with the comment about ZEC leadership culture)

more strongly agree (1 to 5 where 5 is agree most strongly)					
	1	2	3	4	5
Leaders trust each other					
Leaders are valued					
Relationships are valued					
Learning is valued					
Leaders are encouraged to seek guidance					
Diversity of thought is valued					
Innovation is valued					
Continuous improvement is valued					

---

[1] Myles MacBean, "Entrust These to Faithful Men: Towards a Practical Theology for Training Grassroots Preachers in sub-Saharan Africa," *MA Dissertation*, Moorlands College (University of Gloucestershire), 2016. The dissertation may be viewed at www.ptwministry.org.

Appendix A – Quantitative Evaluation Framework

ZEC Context Profile

This section of the evaluation framework was used as part of the guided-questionnaire with ZEC denominational leaders and the training providers that already existed in Malawi and worked with ZEC. This allowed a valuable comparison of internal and external perspectives on ZEC.

Q: Where does ZEC sit on the following dimensions of analysis?

(For the following questions tick the box that best describes the balance of your thinking)

Goals for Preacher Training								
	-3	-2	-1	0	+1	+2	+3	
goals not well defined								goals well defined
not integrated into strategy								integrated into overall ZEC strategy

Context								
	-3	-2	-1	0	+1	+2	+3	
high resource								low resource
urban								rural

Structure								
	-3	-2	-1	0	+1	+2	+3	
formal								informal
centralised								decentralised

Traditional Methods

This section of the evaluation framework was used as part of the guided-questionnaire with ZEC denominational leaders and the training providers. This allowed a valuable comparison between ZEC's perspective and that of the training providers.

Problems with "traditional" methods such as residential college based education.

more important (1 to 5 where 5 is most important)					
	1	2	3	4	5
not training enough people					
not training the right people					
not training people in the right things					

Alternative Methods

This section of the evaluation framework was used as part of the guided-questionnaire with ZEC denominational leaders and the training providers. This allowed a valuable comparison between ZEC's perspective and that of the training providers.

Importance of key components of "alternative" training methods.

more important (1 to 5 where 5 is most important)					
	1	2	3	4	5
home study (cognitive learning)					
practical ministry (field experience)					
seminars (group interaction)					
training conferences (faith community normalisation)					
college integration (integrated education strategy)					

Appendix A – Quantitative Evaluation Framework

Preacher Training

This section of the evaluation framework was used as part of the guided-questionnaire with ZEC denominational leaders and the training providers. This allowed a critical comparison between what ZEC perceived it needed from preacher training and what the training programs aimed to provide.

Q: Where [do ZEC training needs] or [does your training program] sit on the following dimensions of analysis?

(For the following questions tick the box that best describes the balance of your thinking)

Training Profile

	Structure							
	-3	-2	-1	0	+1	+2	+3	
formal								informal
centralised								decentralised

	Curriculum							
	-3	-2	-1	0	+1	+2	+3	
theoretical								applied
scholar								grassroot

	Methodology							
	-3	-2	-1	0	+1	+2	+3	
separated								involved
transmission								discovery

Goals

	1	2	3	4	5
more important (1 to 5 where 5 is most important)					
to form (character, abilities, thought)					
to inform (mind, practice, contemplation)					
to transform (values, people, institutions, communities)					
other (define)					

Principles

	1	2	3	4	5
more important (1 to 5 where 5 is most important)					
contextualisation of theology being taught					
contextualisation of hermeneutic methods being taught					
contextualisation of the homiletic methods being taught					
contextualisation of the training method					
scalability of the training method (sufficient numbers can be trained)					
sustainability of the training method (cost of training affordable)					
Bible centric					
practical and skills based					
coaching/discipleship based					
explicit multiplication (training trainers to train trainers)					
other (define)					

Appendix A – Quantitative Evaluation Framework

Critical Success Factors

This section of the evaluation framework was used as part of the guided-questionnaire with the training providers.

Q: In practice, to what extent has the program demonstrated these selected CSFs?

(For each question tick the box that best describes the extent the CSF has been demonstrated. Be prepared to justify the rating)

	greater extent (increasing from 1 to 5)				
	1	2	3	4	5
training sufficient trainers					
selecting the right trainers					
empowering trainers to innovate					
empowering trainers to train trainers for intentional multiplication					
ensuring ongoing training and coaching for trainers and preachers					
focussing on formation (discipleship) as much as information (teaching)					
developing contextually appropriate content, materials, and methods					
keeping materials and methods simple, low cost, and reproducible					
focussing clearly on who is being trained and what they are being trained					
empowering local leaders to own and contextualise the program					
ensuring integration into the overall strategy of the local church					

Preaching

This section of the evaluation framework was used as part of the guided-questionnaire with ZEC denominational leaders and the training providers. This allowed a critical comparison between what

ZEC perceived its preaching culture to be in terms of the Function/Form of a sermon, versus what the training programs aimed to present as an appropriate preaching culture.

The same questions were used in the self-guided survey of grassroots preachers to evaluate their perception of their individual preaching preferences.

When preparing a sermon, what should a ZEC preacher think about most?

(For each question tick the box that best describes the ideal balance of thinking)

	Function of Sermon							
	-3	-2	-1	0	+1	+2	+3	
helping people understand								helping people grow
pastoring their people								proclaim God's Good News
address people's needs								speaking the message clearly
message from the passage								message from the peoples' needs

	Form of Sermon							
	-3	-2	-1	0	+1	+2	+3	
experiencing God								understanding God
argument								story
philosophy								poetry
feeling								thinking
logic								theatre

Appendix A – Quantitative Evaluation Framework

Learning

This section of the evaluation framework was used as part of the guided-questionnaire within the one-to-one semi-structured interview of a small number of ZEC pastors and church elders. The same questions were used in the self-guided survey of a larger group of grassroots preachers.

To ensure comparability, I used the same list of 40 LSQ questions used by Chris Howles in his research and followed his analytical approach.[2] His 40 questions were in turn based on the work of Peter Honey and Alan Mumford published in 2000.[3]

---

[2] Chris Howles, "African Learning-Style," *BA Dissertation*, Oak Hill Theological College (University of Middlesex), 2010, 29–35.
[3] Peter Honey and Alan Mumford, *The Learning Styles Helpers Guide*, Maidenhead: Peter Honey Publications, 2000.

Appendix B – Selected Results

ZEC Results and Analysis

Context

	N1	N2	N3	R1	R2	R3	Av
Goals							
goals not well defined/ goals well defined	0	-2	-1	-3	3	-3	-1.0
not integrated/ integrated into strategy	-2	-2	-2	-3	3	0	-1.0
Context							
high resource/low resource	0	0	2	3	2	3	1.7
urban/rural	0	3	2	2	3	3	2.2
Structure							
formal/informal	3	0	-2	-3	-3	0	-0.8
centralised/decentralised	0	-2	2	-1	3	1	0.5

Fig. B1 – ZEC Context and Structure

Leadership Culture

	N1	N2	N3	R2	R3	Av
leaders trust each other	2	3	3	4	2	2.8
leaders are valued	3	3	2	5	4	3.4
relationships are valued	5	4	3	4	3	3.8
learning is valued	1	2	2	4	5	2.8
leaders are encouraged to seek guidance	5	2	3	5	4	3.8
diversity of thought is valued	4	2	3	5	4	3.6

Appendix B – Selected Results

innovation is valued	2	3	2	5	3	3.0
continuous improvement is valued	2	3	3	5	4	3.4

Fig. B2 – ZEC Leadership Culture

Churches

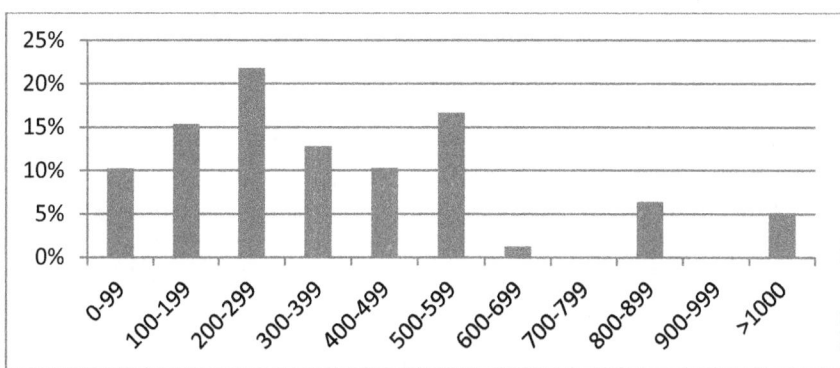

Fig. B3 – Members per Church

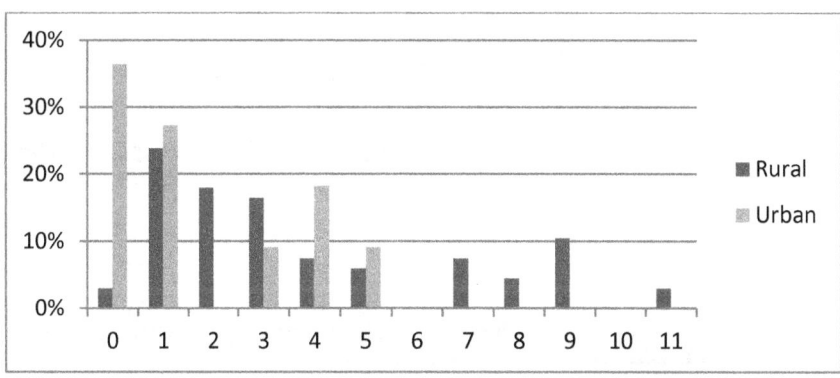

Fig. B4 – Prayer Houses per Church

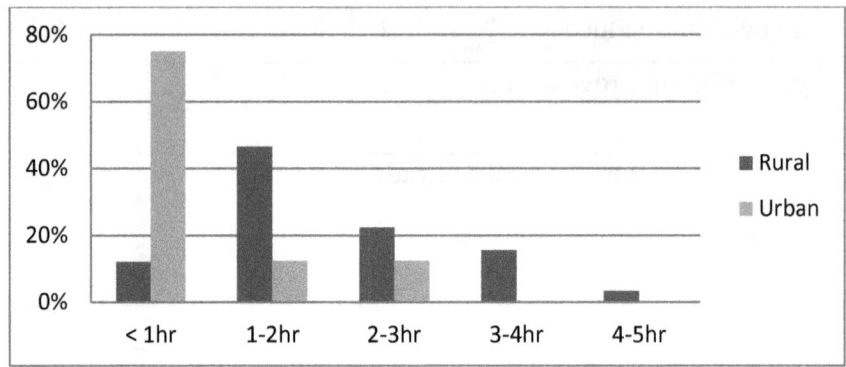

Fig. B5 – Walking Time to Furthest Prayer House

Preachers

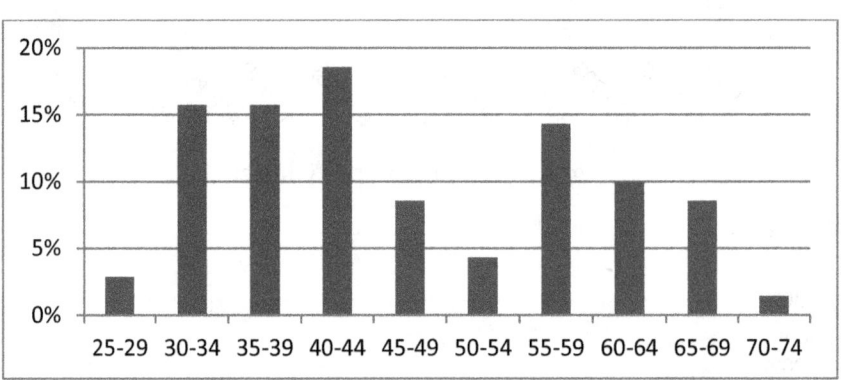

Fig. B6 – Age of Preachers

	College	Secondary	Primary
Elder	15%	55%	31%
Pastor	65%	22%	13%
Total	29%	45%	26%

Fig. B7 – Highest Level of Education

Appendix B – Selected Results

	Mobile	Smart phone	Radio	TV	Computer
rural	70%	9%	48%	28%	4%
urban	64%	18%	64%	82%	9%
all	69%	10%	50%	36%	5%

Fig. B8 – Electronic Devices Available

Preaching

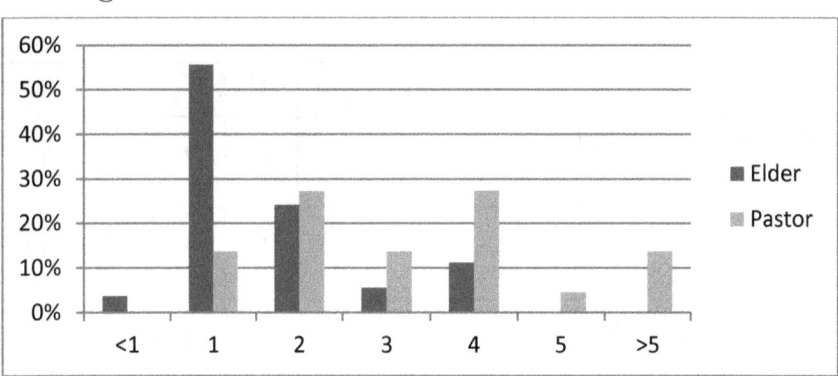

Fig. B9 – How Often in a Month do Preachers Preach

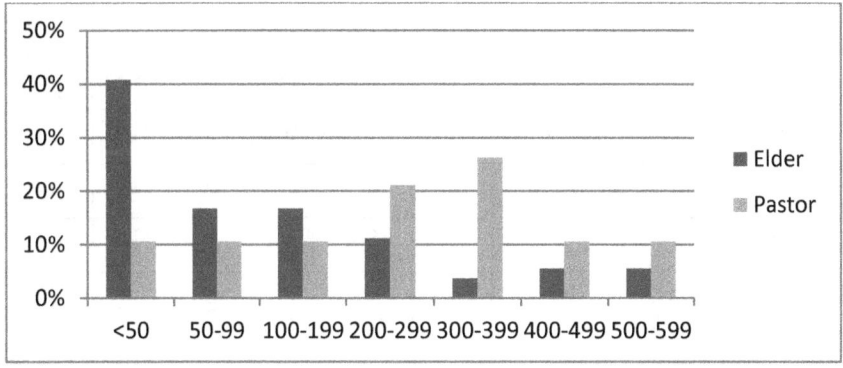

Fig. B10 – How Many People in the Congregation

	Bible	Prayer	Topic	Needs of People	Holy Spirit
Elder	48%	14%	10%	26%	2%
Pastor	24%	30%	6%	41%	0%
Total	41%	19%	8%	31%	2%

Fig. B11 – How do Preachers Decide What to Preach About?

Preacher Training

	N1	N2	N3	R1	R2	R3	Av
not training enough people	4	4	4	4	2	NA	3.6
not training the right people	5	3	3	5	1	NA	3.4
not training people in the right things	2	3	4	1	1	NA	2.2

Fig. B12 – Problems with "Traditional" Methods

	N1	N2	N3	R1	R2	R3	Av
home study	5	4	4	5	5	NA	4.6
practical ministry	5	4	4	5	5	NA	4.6
seminars	3	4	3	5	5	NA	4.0
training conferences	4	4	3	1	5	NA	3.4
college integration	5	4	3	4	5	NA	4.2

Fig. B13 – Key Components of "Alternative" Methods

Appendix B – Selected Results

	N1	N2	N3	R1	R2	R3	Av	Res
Structure								
formal/informal	-3	3	0	-3	-3	0	-1.0	2
centralised/decentralised	1	0	2	3	2	3	1.8	2
Curriculum								
theoretical/applied	3	0	2	3	3	0	1.8	2
scholar/grassroot	3	3	2	3	3	3	2.8	3
Methodology								
separated/involved	2	3	1	3	3	0	2.0	2
transmission/discovery	2	1	0	3	2	0	1.3	2

(Res = researcher's assessment of ZEC)

Fig. B14 – Profile of ZEC Preacher Training Needs

	N1	N2	N3	R1	R2	R3	Av
Goals							
to form	5	5	4	5	5	3	4.5
to inform	5	4	4	5	5	4	4.5
to transform	5	4	5	5	5	5	4.8
Principles							
contextualised theology	4	4	4	4	5	5	4.3
contextualised hermeneutic	5	2	5	5	5	5	4.5
contextualised homiletic	5	3	3	5	5	5	4.3
contextualised training method	5	4	3	5	5	5	4.5
scalability	4	4	4	5	5	5	4.5
sustainability	4	5	4	4	5	5	4.5
Bible centric	5	5	5	5	5	5	5.0
practical and skills based	4	4	4	5	5	5	4.5
coaching/discipleship based	4	5	3	5	5	5	4.5
explicit multiplication	5	5	4	5	5	5	4.8

Fig. B15 – ZEC Training Goals and Principles

Provider Results and Analysis

Qualitative Summary

See Fig. 16 – Summary of Qualitative Results (below).

Appendix B – Selected Results

Prog	Focus	Reach	Course structure	Strengths	Weaknesses
E1	Hermeneutics	Global incl Malawi	4 regional events of 10 days over 2+ years. Non-residential college course.	Proven track record in Malawi. Practical skills focussed. Bible focussed and bible based. Strong on biblical interpretation and communication. Proven scalability. Material in Chichewa. Malawi operation is run by Malawians. Existing relationship with ZEC. Pastor becomes leader/coach.	Global material and model not contextualised. Little emphasis specifically on preaching. Target of trained pastors of aligned with ZEC needs. Risk of material being too academic and literate for preaching elders. Risk of material too expensive for preaching elders.
E2	Discipleship & Bible Study	Global incl Malawi	3 low-intensity village events of 10 days over 1+ year. Frequent local bible studies between.	Proven track record in Malawi. Practical skills focussed. Minimal resource requirement. Bible is text book. Biblical discipleship focussed. Proven scalability. Material highly contextualised and in local language. Existing relationship with ZEC. Church members become disciples and disciple makers. Culture of continuous improvement.	No specific material yet for elders or preachers. Leadership program only evolving. Risk of complex history with ZEC. Not yet coaching between modules. Relatively new charity with limited capacity.
E3	Discipleship & Leadership	Malawi only	4 regional events of 4 days over 2+ years. Interactive teach/train workshops.	Very strong connections with ZEC. Practical skills focussed. Modules go deep into leadership topics. Different learning styles well catered for. Bible interpretation developed through each event.	Little scale yet achieved. Possible conflict of interest through sharing people with ZEC. Not yet any coaching between events. Not yet training trainers. Module with explicit preacher training not available yet.
P1	Preaching & the Preacher	Global/Africa not Malawi	8 regional events of 3-5 days over 4 years. Interactive teach/train workshops.	Proven track record in sub-Saharan Africa, including countries adjacent to Malawi. Strong, practical, preaching oriented curriculum. Demonstrated scale. Demonstrated transition o local movement. Appear flexibility to changing content/structure to match context.	No experience of Malawi. Four year program too long for rural Malawi elders. Probably too costly to be sustainable. English material only. Initial training in English.

Prog	Focus	Reach	Course structure	Strengths	Weaknesses
P2	Preaching & the Preacher	Global/Africa not Malawi	3 events of 4 days over 2+ years. Seminars practice preaching.	Proven track record in sub-Saharan Africa in countries adjacent to Malawi. Homiletics and hermeneutics covered. Recognise need for contextualisation of homiletics and hermeneutics. Powerful, simple and practical training methodology. Training of local trainers is core to methodology. Assumes Bible is all that is available.	No experience of Malawi. Risks assuming basic discipling already done. Risk course too long. Contextualisation of hermeneutic and homiletic models on agenda but not complete. Risk that definition of "expositional" is too narrow for context. Risk that course material too academic for context.
P3	Preaching & the Preacher	Global/Africa not Malawi	3 events of 5 days over 2+ years. Large regional conferences.	Strong focus on expositional preaching. Some success in sub-Saharan Africa. Targets training local trainers to reach rural preachers. Flexibility to contextualisation challenges and review underway. Review of curriculum and methods underway. Desire to introduce coaching model between events.	Not in Malawi for some time. Uncertainty over who target is in future (review underway). Uncertain over what will be taught in future (review underway). Little explicit contextualisation evident in the material. Book set emphasis likely to limit scalability. Curriculum may be too doctrine driven. Emphasis on large conferences not likely feasible in Malawi.
P4	Preaching & the Pastor	African Great Lakes	Non-formal training groups working through 10 modules of 15 units with a trained facilitator.	Proven track record in central Africa. Highly contextualised. Explicit multiplication. Preaching at its core. Built in Africa for Africa. Different learning styles handled well. Coaching model in non-formal groups at its core. Preaching driven curriculum.	Documentation not fully formed. Top tier training is formal and centralised. Program is long with ten modules. Low focus on character formation.

Appendix B – Selected Results

Context

	E1	E2	E3	Av		ZEC
Goals for preacher training						
goals not well defined/goals well defined	-2	-3	-1	-2.0		-1.0
not integrated/integrated into strategy	-1	-3	-1	-1.7		-1.0
Context						
high resource/low resource	3	3	1	2.3		1.7
urban/rural	2	3	2	2.3		2.2
Structure						
formal/informal	2	2	-2	0.7		-0.8
centralised/decentralised	1	-3	-1	-1.0		0.5

Fig. B17 – Program Views of ZEC Context

Preacher Training

	E1	E2	E3	P1	P2	P3	P4		ZEC
not training enough people	4	3	3	3	5	5	5		3.6
not training the right people	5	5	4	4	2	4	2		3.4
not training people in the right things	5	4	3	5	3	4	4		2.2

Fig. B18 – Problems with "Traditional" Methods

	E1	E2	E3	P1	P2	P3	P4	Av	ZEC
home study	3	2	2	4	3	1	3	2.6	4.6
practical ministry	5	5	5	5	4	5	4	4.7	4.6
seminars	5	5	4	5	4	5	5	4.7	4.0
training conferences	4	4	4	1	2	5	2	3.1	3.4
college integration	5	1	2	1	2	2	3	2.3	4.2

Fig. B19 – Key Components of "Alternative" Methods

	E1	E2	E3	P1	P2	P3	P4	ZEC
Context								
high/low resources	-	-	-	1	2	2	2	1.7
urban/rural	-	-	-	-1	1	-1	2	2.2
Structure								
formal/informal	3	3	0	1	3	2	2	-1.0
centralised/ decentralised	3	3	2	-1	2	2	2	1.8
Curriculum								
theoretical/applied	3	3	2	3	3	3	2	1.8
scholar/grassroot	3	3	3	3	3	3	2	2.8
Methodology								
separated/involved	3	3	-1	2	3	2	2	2.0
transmission/discovery	3	3	1	0	2	0	1	1.3

Fig. B20 – Profile of Program Practice

Appendix B – Selected Results

	E1	E2	E3	P1	P2	P3	P4	ZEC
to form	5	5	4	5	5	5	4	4.5
to inform	4	4	2	4	4	5	3	4.5
to transform	5	5	4	3	3	2	5	4.8

Fig. B21 – Goals of the Programs

	E1	E2	E3	P1	P2	P3	P4	ZEC
contextualised theology	5	5	3	1	3	2	4	4.3
contextualised hermeneutic	5	5	2	4	5	2	3	4.5
contextualised homiletic	5	5	3	4	5	3	3	4.3
contextualised training method	5	5	4	4	5	5	5	4.5
scalability	5	5	5	4	5	4	5	4.5
sustainability	5	5	4	4	3	4	5	4.5
Bible centric	5	5	4	5	5	5	5	5.0
practical and skills based	5	5	4	5	5	5	4	4.5
coaching/ discipleship based	5	5	4	5	3	4	3	4.5
explicit multiplication	5	5	4	5	4	4	5	4.8

Fig. B22 – Principles of the Programs

	E1	E2	E3	P1	P2	P3	P4
Training sufficient trainers	5	5	3	3	5	5	3
Selecting the right trainers	5	5	4	4	5	5	2
Empowering trainers to innovate	5	5	3	3	2	3	2
Empowering trainers to train trainers for intentional multiplication	5	5	4	4	4	5	4
Ongoing training and coaching for trainers and preachers	5	5	4	4	4	5	3
Focussing on formation as much as information	5	5	4	5	3	5	2
Contextually appropriate content, materials and methods	5	5	3	3	4	5	4
Materials and methods simple, low cost, and reproducible	5	5	4	2	5	5	3
Clear on who is being trained and what they are being trained	5	5	5	4	4	5	4
Empowering local leaders to own and contextualise the program	4	3	5	4	5	3	4

Appendix B – Selected Results

	E1	E2	E3	P1	P2	P3	P4
Ensuring integration into the overall strategy of the local church	5	5	2	4	2	2	4

Fig. B23 – Critical Success Factors of the Programs

Discussion

Problems with "traditional" methods

	ZEC		Programs	
	Regional	National	Existing	Potential
not training enough people	3.0	4.0	3.3	4.5
not training the right people	3.0	3.7	4.7	3.0
not training people in the right things	1.0	3.0	4.0	4.0

Fig. B24 – Problems with "Traditional" Methods

Key components of "alternative" methods

	ZEC		Programs	
	Regional	National	Existing	Potential
home study	5.0	4.3	2.3	2.8
practical ministry	5.0	4.3	5.0	4.5
seminars	5.0	3.3	4.7	4.8
training conferences	3.0	3.7	4.0	2.5
college integration	4.5	4.0	2.7	2.0

Fig. B25 – Key Components of "Alternative" Methods

Appendix C – Example Session Plans

Overview of Module 1

Day 1 08:30 – 16:30	Day 2 08:30 – 16:00
Model sermon	Model sermon
Introduction to preaching and the preacher	Step 5: Brain Step 6: Heart
Overview of Sculpting Sermons with Scripture. Step 1: Flesh Text 1 (2 Tim 4:1–5)	Understanding orality
Step 2: Skeleton	Step 7: Skeleton
Step 3: Heart Step 4: Brain	Step 8: Flesh
	Practice Text 2 (Titus 1:5–9)
Lunch (13:00)	Lunch (13:00)
Understanding a Bible letter	Participant and trainer short sermon preaching
Practice Text 2 (Titus 1:5–9)	Briefing on journal Feedback form Award certificates

Appendix C — Example Session Plans

Overview of Module 2

	08:30 – 10:30	11:00 – 13:00	14:00 – 14:30
Mon	1 Revision of Module 1		
	Revision M1 (Preach the Word)	Preparation Sermon from a Bible letter (James 1:2–18)	Practice Participants' sermons
Tue	2 Preaching from a story		
	Training Bible Story	Preparation Sermon from a Bible story (Gen 22:1–19)	Practice Participants' sermons
Wed	3 Preaching from poetry		
	Training Bible Poetry	Preparation Sermon from Bible poetry (Psalm 23)	Practice Participants' sermons
Thu	4 Preaching from parables		
	Training Bible Parables	Preparation Sermon from a Bible parable (Matt 13:1–23)	Practice Participants' sermons
Fri	5 Expositional principles 6 Closing	Preaching groups and coaching. Award certificates.	

Module 1: Session 1: Introduction to Preaching and the Preacher

> Objectives of Session 1
>
> In this session you will be introduced to the Preach the Word training program, and learn about the nature and importance of preaching. This gives us the foundations on which the whole training program is based.

1.1 Introduction

Preach the Word is intended to be practical training to "equip and release" preachers. There will be lots of practice built into the program.

By the end of Module 1 you will understand the practical principles of preaching and finish the course being able to give a short sermon that:

- identifies the original message within the original context of a Bible passage;
- effectively communicates that meaning to today's audience in a sub-Saharan context;
- appropriately applies the message so that the listener is given something to think, believe, decide, and do.

It is important that you take good notes in your own words as this will help you remember and continue learning over the coming months.

Pay attention in every session as each one is important and builds on the previous one.

1.2 Preaching as a Craft

In understanding the approach we are taking to preaching, it is important to recognize that preaching is a 'craft' involving both 'gifts' we are born with and 'skills' we learn through practice. We get into trouble if we don't get the balance right.

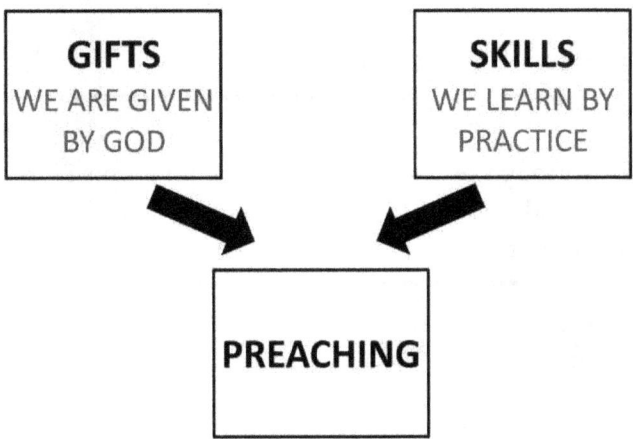

You will have lots of opportunity to practice during the course but you must realize that an expert craftsman typically requires 10,000 hours of practice. This course must be the start of years of reflective practice.

1.3 Importance of Preaching

Preaching is vitally important in principle because of the emphasis given to it in Scripture. For example, in 2 Timothy 4:1, Paul gives Timothy the solemn charge to "Preach the Word." Also, Jesus and his disciples gave significant priority to preaching (e.g. Matthew 5, Acts 6, Romans 10:14–19).

Preaching is also vitally important in practice because in our oral Malawi culture, with so few Bibles, preaching is often the only way many Christians hear God's Word.

1.4 Nature of Preaching

1.4.1 Genesis 1:3 and Romans 15:4

> **Discover**
>
> Break into groups of 2 or 3. Spend 5 minutes considering what Genesis 1:3 and Romans 15:4 tell us about the nature of preaching. Be prepared to report back to the class.

We find that:

- God is a speaking God (Genesis 1:3);
- He spoke in the past ("everything that was written in the past");
- And "everything written in the past was written to teach us;"
- That lives might be changed ("so that ... we might have hope.")

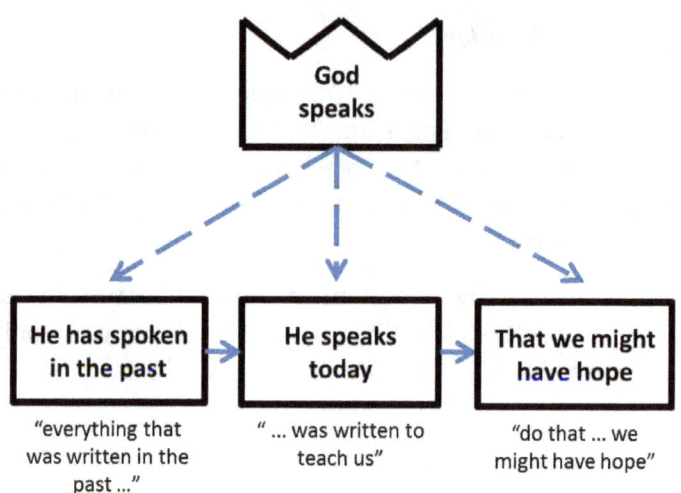

[Based on BUILD Module 1, Unit 2]

Appendix C — Example Session Plans

1.4.2 2 Timothy 4:1–5

> Discover
>
> Break into groups of 3 or 4. Spend 5 minutes considering what 2 Timothy 4:1–5 tells us about the nature of preaching, the character of the preacher, and what we can expect to face as preachers. Be prepared to report back to the class.

We find that:

We are called/appointed to preach (v. 1).

We should be ready to preach at all times in all circumstances ("in season and out," v. 2).

We should have content that is well considered "careful instruction" (v. 2).

We should have an attitude and tone of "great patience" (v. 2).

We should aim to reach the mind ("correct"), the will ("rebuke"), the heart ("encourage") (v. 2)

We should preach "sound doctrine" (v. 3) and "truth" (v. 4).

However, we will be working among false teachers selling "myth" (v. 4).

Nevertheless, we must keep our heads and "endure hardship" (v. 5).

1.5 Expository Preaching

1.5.1 A Definition

Pulling all this together we find that the fundamental foundation of true preaching can be seen to be 'exposition'. This is not a particular style of preaching but a principle:

1.5.2 Three Principles

We can also derive three principles that we will keep in mind throughout the course:

Principle 1: We get the meaning from the Bible passage, we don't bring the meaning to the Bible passage.

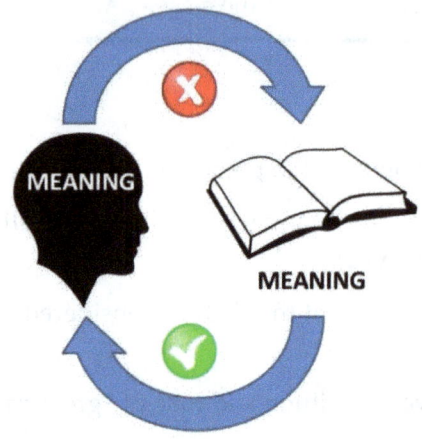

Principle 2: The Bible passage is not the diving rock for our sermon, it is the lake that we swim in throughout our sermon.

Principle 3: At its core, preaching is a work of the Holy Spirit working through the character and personality of the preacher. We need to be people of mature biblical character, saturation prayer, deep Bible familiarity, and a reflective spirit.

Appendix C — Example Session Plans

> Summary of key points from Session 1
>
> Preaching is a craft that brings together gifts we are born with and skills we practice. The Bible demonstrates the importance of preaching in principle through the example of Jesus and the disciples.
>
> Preaching is also vitally important in practice because of our oral culture in Malawi.
>
> A Biblical definition of preaching is:
>
> exposing the original meaning of a Bible passage to its original audience in its original context
>
> communicating that meaning to today's audience in today's context so that the Holy Spirit might change lives.
>
> There are three key principles to remember when we preach:
>
> We get the meaning from the Bible passage we don't bring the meaning to the Bible passage.
>
> The Bible passage is not the diving rock for our sermon, it is the lake that we swim in throughout our sermon.
>
> Preaching is a work of the Holy Spirit working through the character and personality of the preacher.

Module 1 – Session 5: Understanding a Bible Letter

> **Objectives of Session 5**
>
> The Bible contains many different types of writing. In this session you will learn about particular characteristics of a Bible letter. This will help you better identify the message of a passage in a Bible letter, and understand the purpose of the original author.

5.1 *The Style of the Bible Passage*

Letters are only one of many styles of Bible writing, with each style requiring slightly different approaches if we are to understand the true meaning of the passage in its original context.

Bible styles include: letter (or epistle, e.g. Romans), genealogies (e.g. Genesis 5), historical narrative (e.g. Acts), law (e.g. Leviticus), parable (e.g. Luke 18:9–14), poetry (e.g. Psalms), proverbs/wisdom (e.g. Proverbs), and prophecy (e.g. Daniel).

More simply, forms of Bible writing can be thought of as ideas based, story based, or poetry based (where the structure or sound of the words enhances meaning).

Bible letters are good examples of ideas based Bible writing.

5.2 *Characteristics of a Letter*

> **Practice**
>
> Break into groups of 3 or 4 people. Spend 10 minutes considering the characteristics and purpose of a normal letter (not a Bible letter) as a communications tool. Be prepared to report back to the class on what you find.

5.3 Bible Letters

Letters have always been a very common form of writing and are closest to spoken conversation. They are personal and immediate and directed at a particular set of circumstances for a particular individual or group.

A Bible letter is just the same. They also have a certain stylized form and typically have a **beginning** that identifies the author and expresses a friendly relationship. The letter as a whole brings the writer into some form of **emotional presence** with the reader, often the emotion of thanksgiving. The body of the letter creates a **dialogue** between sender and receiver, usually about doctrinal or ethical matters. The **closing** often reiterates the key points of the letter.

Letters are like a face-to-face encounter but the author is often free to express themselves more energetically, plainly, and forcefully in a letter than they might in an oral conversation. Some things are "easier to put in a letter".

On the other hand, the person receiving the letter can reject the message in the letter without rejecting the person writing the letter.

In summary, concerning letters:

They are **from** someone, **to** someone, **with** a message (or messages), and **for** a purpose (or for several purposes).

They are written on a particular occasion for a particular reason. That is why it is important to discover the **situation** or context the letter was written for.

They **explain** and **apply** Christian truth to real life situations.

5.4 Sculpting a Sermon with a Bible Letter

Understanding these specific characteristics will help us as we prepare a sermon from a passage in a Bible letter, and leave us better able to identify the message of the Bible passage and understand the purpose of the original author.

Because Bible letters were intentionally written to convey a message for a purpose they are often the easiest type of Bible writing from which to identify the message and understand the purpose.

> Practice
>
> Break into groups of 3 or 4 people. Spend 20 minutes analysing the Bible letter of Philemon. Identify in Philemon as many as possible of the characteristics of a Bible letter. Be prepared to report back to the class on what you find.

> Summary of key points from Session 5
>
> Bible letters are an example of an ideas-based Bible writing style
>
> They have many characteristics that are the same as a modern letter or emails.
>
> They are from someone, to someone, with a message, and for a purpose.
>
> They were written on a particular occasion, in a particular context, and explain/apply Christian truth to real life situations.
>
> Understanding these particular characteristics will help us identify the message of a passage in a Bible letter, and understand the purpose of the original author.

Bibliography

Adeyemo, Tokunboh, Ed. *Africa Bible Commentary,* Grand Rapids: Zondervan, 2010.

Allen, Robert A. "The Expository Sermon: Cultural or Biblical." *Journal of Ministry and Theology* 2:2 (1998): 212–220.

Anderson, James A. "Cognitive Style and Multicultural Populations." *Journal of Teacher Education* 39:1 (1988): 2–9.

Anderson, Kenton C. *Choosing to Preach: A Comprehensive Introduction to Sermon Options and Structures.* Grand Rapids: Zondervan, 2006.

Arnold, Jackie. *Coaching Skills for Leaders in the Workplace: How to Develop, Motivate and Get the Best from Your Staff.* Oxford: How to Books, 2010.

Ash, Christopher. *The Priority of Preaching.* Fearn: Christian Focus, 2009.

Banda, Kelvin N. *A Brief History of Education in Malaŵi.* Blantyre: Dzuka Publishing Company, 1982.

Batlle, Agustin, and Rosario Batlle. "Theological Community of Chile: Extension Training for Indigenous Church Leaders." Pages 61–67 in F. Ross Kinsler, ed. *Ministry by the People: Theological Education by Extension,* Geneva: WCC, 1983.

Bell, Judith. *Doing Your Research Project: A Guide for First-time Researchers in Education, Health and Social Science.* Maidenhead: McGraw-Hill Education, 2010.

Bowen, Dorothy N., and Earle A. Bowen. "Contextualisation of Teaching Methodology in Theological Education." *Conference of Theological Educators, Limuru, Kenya,* 1988: 1–13.

Bowers, Paul. "Theological Education in Africa: Why Does It Matter?" *African Journal of Evangelical Theology,* 26:2 (2007): 135–149.

van Breugel, J. W. M. *Chewa Traditional Religion.* Blantyre: CLAIM, 2001.

Burton, Sam Westman. *Disciple Mentoring: Theological Education by Extension.* Pasadena, CA: William Carey Library, 2000.

Cahill, Dennis M. *The Shape of Preaching: Theory and Practice in Sermon Design.* Grand Rapids: Baker, 2007.

Cairns, Earle. *Preach the Word!* Maitland: Xulon Press, 2005.

Caple, Jim, and Paul Martin. "Reflections of Two Pragmatists: A Critique of Honey and Mumford's Learning Styles." *Industrial and Commerical Training*, 26:1 (1994): 16–20.

Carson, D. A., and Timothy J. Keller. *Gospel-Centered Ministry*. Wheaton, IL: Crossway, 2011.

Cartledge, Mark J. *Practical Theology: Charismatic and Empirical Perspectives*. Eugene, OR: Wipf & Stock, 2012.

Castro, Emilio. "Foreword." Pahes ix–xii in F. Ross Kinsler, ed. *Ministry by the People: Theological Education by Extension*, Geneva: WCC, 1983.

Chakanza, J. C. *Initiation Rites for Boys in Lomwe Society in Malawi and Other Essays*. Zomba: Kachere Series, 2005.

Chapell, Bryan. *Christ-Centered Preaching: Redeeming the Expository Sermon*. 2nd ed. Grand Rapids: Baker Academic, 2005.

Chifungo, Davidson Kamayaya. "An Oral Hermeneutics within the Lay Preaching Context of the Nkhoma Synod of the Church of Central Africa Presbyterian (CCAP): A Critical Evaluation." PhD, Stellenbosch University, 2013.

Coffield, Frank, David Moseley, Elaine Hall, and Kathryn Eccleston. *Learning Styles and Pedagogy in Post-16 Learning: A Systematic and Critical Review*. London: The Learning and Skills Research Centre, 2004.

Collins, Gary R. *Christian Coaching: Helping Others Turn Potential into Reality*. Colorado Springs: NavPress, 2001.

Costas, Orlando E., "Theological Education and Mission." in C. Rene Padilla, ed. *New Alternatives in Theological Education*, Oxford: Regnum, 1988.

Craddock, Fred B. *As One Without Authority: Fourth Edition Revised and with New Sermons*. Atlanta: Chalice, 2001.

Creswell, Jane. *Christ-Centered Coaching: 7 Benefits for Ministry Leaders*. Atlanta: Chalice, 2006.

Creswell, John W. *Research Design: Qualitative, Quantitative, and Mixed Method Approaches*. 2nd ed. Thousand Oaks, CA: Sage, 2003.

Cronshaw, Darren. "Re-envisioning Theological Education, Mission and the Local Church." *Mission Studies*, 28 (2011): 91–115.

Day, David. "Six Feet Above Contradiction? An Overview." Pages 1–7 in David Day, Jeff Astley, and Leslie J. Francis, eds. *A Reader On Preaching: Making Connections*. Aldershot: Ashgate, 2005.

Bibliography and Endnotes

Denscombe, Martyn. *Ground Rules For Social Research: Guidelines for Good Practice*. Maidenhead: McGraw-Hill International, 2009.

Denscombe, Martyn. *The Good Research Guide*. Maidenhead: McGraw-Hill International, 2007.

Denzin, Norman K. *The Research Act: A Theoretical Introduction to Sociological Methods*. Chicago, IL: Aldine, 1970.

Denzin, Norman K., and Yvonna S. Lincoln. "Introduction: The Discipline and Practice of Qualitative Research." Pages 1–20 in Norman K. Denzin and Yvonna S. Lincoln, eds. *The SAGE Handbook of Qualitative Research*. London: Sage, 2011.

Downey, Myles. *Effective Coaching: Lessons from the Coaches' Coach*. 2nd ed. New York; London: Texere, 2003.

Fairholm, Gilbert W. *Leadership and the Culture of Trust*. Westport: Greenwood, 1994.

Ferris, Robert W. "The Future of Theological Education." in Robert L. Youngblood. *Cyprus: TEE Come of Age*. Exeter: Paternoster, 1986.

Fiedler, Klaus. *The Story of Faith Missions*. Oxford: Regnum, 1994.

Fulop, Christina. "History and Development." Pages 22–43 in Conrad Lashley and Alison J. Morrison, eds. *Franchising Hospitality Services*. The Hospitality, Leisure and Tourism Series. Oxford: Butterworth, 2000.

Germann, Stewart. "Franchise Right." *Chartered Accountants Journal*, (April 2009): 72–74.

Graetz, Fiona, Malcolm Rimmer, Aaron Smith, and Ann Lawrence. *Managing Organisational Change*. 3rd ed. Milton, NSW: John Wiley & Sons Australia, 2012.

Groves, Jonathan D. *Reading Romans at Ground Level: A Contemporary Rural African Perspective*. Carlisle: Langham Global Library, 2015.

Guild, Pat. "The Culture/Learning Style Connection." *Educating for Diversity* 51:8 (1994): 16–21.

Harkavy, Daniel. *Becoming a Coaching Leader: The Proven Strategy for Building a Team of Champions*. Nashville, TN: Nelson Business, 2007.

Harrison, Patricia J. "Forty Years On: The Evolution of Theology by Extension." *Evangelical Review of Theology* 28:4 (2004): 315–328.

Hawkins, Tim. *Messages That Move*. Epsom: The Good Book Company, 2013.

Hobson, Andy. "Mentoring and Coaching for New Leaders: Summary Report." National College for School Leadership, 2003.

Holland, Fred. "TEXT Africa: Programming for Ministry Through Theological Education by Extension." Pages 103–115 in F. Ross Kinsler, ed. *Ministry by the People: Theological Education by Extension*. Geneva: WCC, 1983.

Honey, Peter. *The Learning Styles Questionnaire: 40-Item Version*. London: Pearson Clinical and Talent Assessment, 2006.

Honey, Peter and Alan Mumford. *The Learning Styles Helper's Guide*. Maidenhead: Peter Honey, 2000.

Honey, Peter, and Alan Mumford. *The Learning Styles Helper's Guide*. Maidenhead: Peter Honey, 2006.

Hovil, R. Jeremy. G. "An Investigation into Alternative and Appropriate Models of Theological Education for Non-Western Contexts." *MTh Dissertation*, Spurgeon's College (University of Wales), 1999.

Hovil, R. Jeremy. G. "Transforming Theological Education in the Church of the Province of Uganda (Anglican)." D.Th, University of Stellenbosch, 2005.

Hovil, R. J. G. "The Advantages and Disadvantages of Different Models of Training." *Trust in Christ Consultation*. Bath, 2001: 1–37.

Hovil, R. J. G., A. E. Carl, and H. J. Hendriks. "The Promise of Dynamic Curriculum Development Models for Transforming Multi-Level Systems of Theological Education: A Ugandan Case Study." *Dutch Reformed Theological Journal* 47: 3&4 (2006): 534–546.

Howles, Chris. "African Learning-Style." *BA Dissertation for "Theology and World Mission."* Oak Hill Theological College (University of Middlesex), 2010.

Hunt, James M., and Joseph R. Weintraub. *The Coaching Organization: A Strategy for Developing Leaders*. London: Sage, 2006.

Hussey, David E. *How to Manage Organisational Change*. London: Kogan Page, 2000.

Jenkins, Philip. *The New Faces of Christianity: Believing the Bible in the Global South*. New York: Oxford University Press, 2006.

Johnstone, Patrick, and Jason Mandryk. *Operation World: 21st Century Edition*. Milton Keynes: Paternoster, 2001.

Joy, Simy, and David A. Kolb. "Are There Cultural Differences in Learning Style?" *International Journal of Intercultural Relations* 1:33 (2009): 69–85.

Kalinga, Owen J. M. *Historical Dictionary of Malawi*. Lanham: Rowman & Littlefield, 2012.

Kapteina, Detlef. "The Formation of African Evangelical Theology." *Africa Journal of Evangelical Theology* 25:1 (2006): 61–84.

Kinsler, F. Ross, ed. *Ministry by the People: Theological Education by Extension*. Geneva: WCC, 1983.

Kinsler, F. Ross. "Preface." Pages xiii–xvi in F. Ross Kinsler, ed. *Ministry by the People: Theological Education by Extension*. Geneva: WCC, 1983.

Kinsler, F. Ross. "Theological Education by Extension: Equipping God's People for Ministry." Pages 1–29 in F. Ross Kinsler, ed. *Ministry by the People: Theological Education by Extension*. Geneva: WCC, 1983.

Kinsler, Ross. "Doing Ministry for a Change: Theological Education for the Twenty-First Century." *Ministerial Formation* 108 (2007): 4–13.

Kisau, Paul. "The Key to the African Heart: Rethinking Missionary Strategy in Africa." *Africa Journal of Evangelical Theology* 17:2 (1998): 85–105.

Kohls, Paul. "A Look at Church Leadership in Africa." *Africa Journal of Evangelical Theology* 17:2 (1998): 107–126.

Kolb, Alice Y., and David A. Kolb. *The Kolb Learning Style Inventory. Version 3.1: 2005*. Boston and London: Hay Resources Direct, 2005.

Kolb, David A. *Experiential Learning: Experience as the Source of Learning and Development*. Englewood Cliffs: Prentice Hall, 1984.

Kotter, John P. "Leading Change: Why Transformation Efforts Fail." *Harvard Business Review* 85:1 (2000): 96–103.

Lashley, Conrad. "Empowered Franchisees?" Pages 68–91 in Conrad Lashley and Alison J. Morrison, ed. *Franchising Hospitality Services*. The Hospitality, Leisure and Tourism Series. Oxford; Boston: Butterworth/Heinemann, 2000).

Light, David A. "Franchising." *Harvard Business Review* 75:3 (1997): 14–15.

Lloyd-Jones, David Martyn. *Preaching and Preachers*. London: Hodder and Stoughton, 1971.

Long, Thomas G. "A New Focus for Teaching Preaching." Pages 3–17 in Thomas G. Long and Leonora Tubbs Tisdale, eds. *Teaching Preaching as a Christian Practice: A New Approach to Homiletic Pedagogy*. Louisville, KY: Westminster John Knox, 2008.

Long, Thomas G. "The Distance We Have Travelled: Changing Trends in Preaching." Pages 11–16 in David Day, Jeff Astley, and Leslie J. Francis, eds. *A Reader On Preaching: Making Connections.* Aldershot: Ashgate, 2005.

Long, Thomas G. *The Witness of Preaching.* 2nd ed. Louisville, KY: Westminster John Knox, 2005.

Lowry, Eugene L. *Homiletical Plot: The Sermon as Narrative Art Form.* Expanded Edition. Louisville, KY: Westminster John Knox, 2000.

Lowry, Eugene L. *How to Preach a Parable: Designs for Narrative Sermons.* Nashville, TN: Abingdon, 1989.

Lowry, Eugene L. "The Revolution of Sermonic Shape." Pages 93–112 in Gail R. O'Day and Thomas G. Long, eds. *Listening to the Word: Studies in Honor of Fred B. Craddock.* Nashville, TN: Abingdon, 1993.

Mbewe, Conrad. *Pastoral Preaching: Building a People for God.* Carlisle: Langham, 2017.

MacBean, Myles. "The Homiletic Window." *Evangelical Review of Theology* 41:3 (2017): 209–21.

Maitland, Iain. *Franchising: A Practical Guide for Franchisors and Franchisees.* Winnipeg, MB: Mercury, 1991.

Marah, John K. "The Virtues and Challenges in Traditional African Education." *The Journal of Pan African Studies* 1:4 (2006): 15–24.

McCracken, John. *A History of Malawi, 1859–1966.* Woodbridge: Boydell & Brewer, 2012.

Mesters, Carlos. "Bible Study Centre for People's Pastoral Action (Brazil): The Use of the Bible Among the Common People." Pages 78–92 in F. Ross Kinsler, ed. *Ministry by the People: Theological Education by Extension,* Geneva: WCC, 1983.

Miller, Linda J., and Chad W. Hall. *Coaching for Christian Leaders: A Practical Guide,* Atlanta. GA: Chalice, 2007.

Morrison, Alison J. "Entrepreneurs or Intrapeneurs?" Pages 68–91 in Conrad Lashley and Alison J. Morrison, eds. *Franchising Hospitality Services,* The Hospitality, Leisure and Tourism Series, Oxford: Butterworth, 2000.

Morrison, Philip E. "Implications of Paul's Model for Leadership Training in Light of Church Growth in Africa." *Evangelical Review of Theology* 30:1 (2011): 55–71.

Motyer, J. A. *Preaching? Simple Teaching on Simply Preaching*. Fearn: Christian Focus, 2013.

Moyce, Cliff. "Culture Change." *Management Services* 59:1 (2015): 28–30.

Mshana, Bumija, and Dean Paterson. "Lutheran Synod and Roman Catholic Diocese of Arusha: Training Village Ministries in Tanzania." Pages 127–134 in F. Ross Kinsler, ed. *Ministry by the People: Theological Education by Extension*. Geneva: WCC, 1983.

Mulholland, Kenneth B., and Kelly de Jacobs. "Presbeterian Seminary of Guatemala: A Modest Experiment Becomes a Model for Change." Pages 33–41 in F. Ross Kinsler, ed. *Ministry by the People: Theological Education by Extension*. Geneva: WCC, 1983.

Munoz-Seca, Beatriz, and Cassia Silva Santiago. "Four Dimensions to Induce Learning: The Challenge Profile." IESE Business School, University of Navarra, 2003.

Newbigin, Leslie. "Theological Education in a World Perspective." *Churchman* 94:2, 1979: 105–115.

Nhiwatiwa, Eben K. *Preaching in the African Context: How We Preach*. Nashville, TN: Langham, 2012.

Nhiwatiwa, Eben K. *Preaching in the African Context: Why We Preach*. Nashville, TN: Langham, 2012.

O'Connor, John Patrick. *Reproducible Pastoral Training: Church Planting Guidelines from the Teachings of George Patterson*. Pasadena, CA: William Carey Library, 2006.

Ogne, Steven L. *TransforMissional Coaching: Empowering Spiritual Leaders in a Changing Ministry World*. Nashville, TN: B&H, 2008.

Olford, Stephen F., and David L. Olford. *Anointed Expository Preaching*. Nashville, TN: B&H, 1998.

One Mission Society, "Village Church Planting," *Into Africa Project*, <http://www.intoafricaproject.org/vcp/index.html>.

Orridge, Martin. *Change Leadership: Developing a Change-Adept Organization*. Farnham: Gower, 2012.

Ott, Craig. *Encountering Theology of Mission: Biblical Foundations, Historical Developments, and Contemporary Issues*. Encountering Mission. Grand Rapids: Baker Academic, 2010.

Ott, Craig, and Gene Wilson. *Global Church Planting: Biblical Principles and Best Practices for Multiplication*. Grand Rapids: Baker, 2011.

Pachai, Bridglal. *Malawi; the History of the Nation*. Harlow: Longman, 1973.

Para-Mallam, Gideon. "Theological Trends in Africa: Implications for Missions and Evangelism." *Lausanne Reports*, 03, 2008.

Parker, Shane. "The Supervisor as Mentor-Coach in Theological Field Education." *Christian Education Journal* 6:1 (2009): 51–63.

Pathak, Harsh. *Organisational Change*. New Delhi: Pearson, 2010.

Patterson, George. "Foreword." Pages xv–xvi in John Patrick O'Connor. *Reproducible Pastoral Training: Church Planting Guidelines from the Teachings of George Patterson*. Pasadena: William Carey Library, 2006.

Pauw, Christoff Martin. *The History of the Nkhoma Synod of the Church of Central Africa, Presbyterian, 1889–1962*. Lusaka: Church of Central Africa Presbyterian, 1962.

Phiri, D. D. *History of Malawi: From Earliest Times to the Year 1915*. Blantyre: CLAIM, 2004.

Pike, John G. "A Pre-Colonial History of Malawi." *The Nyasaland Journal* 18:1, 1965: 22–54.

Prime, Derek J., and Alistair Begg. *On Being A Pastor: Understanding Our Calling and Work*, Chicago, IL: Moody, 2004.

Pritchard, John, and Paul Ballard. *Practical Theology in Action: Christian Thinking in the Service of Church and Society*. London: SPCK, 2006.

Project Worldreach, *Train and Multiply*. <http://www.trainandmultiply.com/>.

Rafael, B. R. *A Short History of Malawi*. Limbe: Popular, 1988.

Reid, Robert Stephen. "Postmodernism and the Function of the New Homiletic in Post-Christendom Congregations." *Homiletic* 20:2 (1995): 1–13.

Richard, Ramesh. *Scripture Sculpture: A Do-It-Yourself Manual for Biblical Preaching*. Grand Rapids: Baker, 1995.

Robinson, Haddon W. *Biblical Preaching: The Development and Delivery of Expository Messages*. Grand Rapids: Baker Academic, 2001.

Robinson, Haddon W. *Expository Preaching: Principles & Practice*. Leicester: Inter-Varsity, 2001.

Robson, Colin. *How to Do a Research Project: A Guide for Undergraduate Students.* 1st edition. Malden: John Wiley & Sons, 2007.

Robson, Colin. *Real World Research: A Resource for Social Scientists and Practitioner-Researchers.* 2nd edition. Oxford: John Wiley & Sons, 2002.

Roth, George L., and Anthony J. DiBella. *Systemic Change Management: The Five Capabilities for Improving Enterprises.* London: Palgrave Macmillan, 2015.

Sadler-Smith, Eugene. "Cognitive Style and Learning in Organisations." Pages 181–208 in Riding, R. J., and Stephen G. Rayner, eds. *International Perspectives on Individual Differences, Volume 1: Cognitive Styles,* Stamford, CT: Ablex, 2000.

Sales, Richard, and Jacob Liphoko. "Grassroots Theology in Botswana." Pages 135–147 in F. Ross Kinsler, ed. *Ministry by the People: Theological Education by Extension.* Geneva: WCC, 1983.

Sangster, W. E. *The Craft of Sermon Construction.* London: Pickering and Inglis, 1978.

Sangster, W. E. *The Craft of the Sermon.* London: Epworth Press, 1954.

Sawyer, Clive. *How to Franchise Your Business: The Plain-Speaking Guide for Business Owners.* London: Live It, 2011.

Scanlon, David G. "Conflicting Traditions in African Education." Pages 1–12 in David G. Scanlon, ed. *Traditions of African Education,* New York: Columbia University, 1964.

Schein, Edgar H. *Organizational Culture and Leadership.* Oxford: John Wiley & Sons, 2010.

Scott, Shane, and Chester Spell. "Factors for New Franchise Success." *Sloan Management Review* 39:3 (1998): 43–50.

Sills, Michael David. "Training Leaders for the Majority World Church in the 21st Century." *Global Missiology English* 3:1 (2004): 171–186.

Smith, Gordon W., Bridglal Pachai, and Roger K. Tangri. Malawi Past and Present: Selected Papers from the University of Malawi History Conference. Blantyre: CLAIM, 1971.

Smith, Steve. *T4T: A Discipleship Re-Revolution.* Monument, CO: WIGTake Resources, 2011.

Stavredes, Tina. *Effective Online Teaching: Foundations and Strategies for Student Success.* Oxford: John Wiley & Sons, 2011.

Steffen, Tom A. *The Facilitator Era: Beyond Pioneer Church Multiplication.* Eugene, OR: Wipf and Stock, 2011.

Stoltzfus, Tony. *Leadership Coaching: The Disciplines, Skills and Heart of a Christian Coach.* Virginia Beach, VA: Coach22, 2005.

Stott, John R. W. *I Believe in Preaching.* London: Hodder and Stoughton, 1982.

Strong, David K., and Cynthia A. Strong. "The Globalizing Hermeneutic of the Jerusalem Council." Pages 127–139 in Craig Ott and Harold Netland, eds. *Globalizing Theology: Belief and Practice in an Era of World Christianity.* Grand Rapids: Baker Academic, 2006.

Sugars, Bradley J. *Successful Franchising: Expert Advice on Buying, Selling and Creating Winning Franchises.* 1st Edition. New York: McGraw-Hill, 2006.

Swinton, John, and Harriet Mowatt. *Practical Theology and Qualitative Research Methods.* London: SCM Press, 2006.

Taylor, Stephen. "An Introduction." Pages 3–21 in Conrad Lashley and Alison J. Morrison, eds. *Franchising Hospitality Services.* The Hospitality, Leisure and Tourism Series. Oxford: Butterworth, 2000.

Thomas, Gary. *How To Do Your Research Project: A Guide for Students in Education and Applied Social Sciences.* 2nd Edition. Thousand Oaks, CA: Sage, 2013.

Tienou, Tite. "Contextualisation of Theology for Theological Education." Pages 42–52 in Paul Bowers, ed. *Evangelical Theological Education Today: 2. An Agenda for Renewal.* Nairobi: Evangel, 1982.

Turley, Phillip. "Extending the Fence: Suggestions for the Future of TEE in Africa." *Africa Journal of Evangelical Theology* 10:1 (1991): 39–52.

van der Ven, Johannes A. "An Empirical or a Normative Approach to Practical-Theological Research? A False Dilemma." *Journal of Empirical Theology,* 15:2 (2002): 5–33.

Vajko, Robert J. "The Transformation of Society by Planting New Churches." *Ogbomoso Journal of Theology* 16:3 (2011): 95–114.

Vibert, Simon. *Excellence in Preaching: Learning from the Best.* Nottingham: Inter-Varsity, 2011.

De Vita, Glauco. "Learning Styles, Culture and Inclusive Instruction in the Multicultural Classroom: A Business and Management Perspective." *Innovations in Education and Teaching International* 38:2 (2001): 165–171.

Walliman, Nicholas. *Your Research Project: A Step-by-Step Guide for the First-Time Researcher.* 2nd Edition. London: Sage, 2005.

Wambua, Serah. "Mission Spirituality and Authentic Discipleship: An African Reflection." *Seoul Consultation, Study Commission IX.* Seoul; Edinburgh (2009, 2010): 45–54.

Wendland, Ernst, and Salimo Hachibamba. *Galu Wamkota: Missiological Reflections from South – Central Africa.* Zomba: Kachere Series, 2007.

West, Russell W. "Church-Based Theological Education: When the Seminary Goes back to Church." *Journal of Religious Leadership* 2:2 (2003): 113–165.

Wilhelm, Dawn Ottoni. "New Hermeneutic, Hew Homiletic, and New Directions: An U.S.-North American Perspective." *Homiletic (Online)* 35:1 (2010): 17–23.

Williams, Howard. *My Word.* Norwich: SCM, 1973.

Willimon, William H., and Richard Lischer, eds. *Concise Encyclopedia of Preaching.* Louisville, KY: Westminster John Knox, 1995.

Wilson, Carol. *Best Practice in Performance Coaching: A Handbook for Leaders, Coaches, HR Professionals and Organizations.* 1st Edition. London: Kogan Page, 2011.

Winter, Ralph D. *Frontiers in Mission: Discovering and Surmounting Barriers to the Missio Dei.* Pasadena, CA: William Carey International University Press, 2008.

Winter, Ralph D. "The Largest Stumbling Block to Leadership Development in the Global Church." *International Journal of Frontier Missions* 20:3 (2003): 86–94.

Young, Mark. "What Forms of Theological Education Are Appropriate for Post-Communist Europe?" A Paper Consultation on Theological Education and Leadership Development in Post-Communist Europe. Oradea, Romania, October 4–8th, 1994.

Zorn, Herbert M. *Viability in Context: A Study of the Financial Viability of Theological Education in the Third World – Seedbed or Sheltered Garden?* Bromley: WCC, 1973.

Zokoue, Isaac. "Educating for Servant Leadership in Africa." *Africa Journal of Evangelical Theology* 9:1 (1990): 3–13.

BUILD Curriculum. <http://www.buildcurriculum.org>

BUILD Partners. <http://buildpartners.org>

"Country – Malawi." *Joshua Project.* <http://joshuaproject.net/ countries/ MI>.

Country Reports: Malawi. Country Report. IHS Global Inc., 2015.

"Editorial: Empty Hearts and Empty Minds." *Africa Journal of Evangelical Theology* 117:2 (1998): 83–84.

Quenum, Jean-Marie Hyacinthe. "Growing up and Maturing in African Perspective." *Academia* (n.d.): 1–27. <https://www.academia.edu/1533345/GrowingupandMaturinginAfricanPerspective>.

"Human Development Index and Its Components | Human Development Reports." *United Nations Development Programme.* <http://hdr.undp.org/en/content/table-1-human-development-index-and-its-components>.

"Malawi | Data." *World Bank.* <http://data.worldbank.org/country/ Malawi>.

"Malawi | Operation World." *Operation World.* <http://www.operationworld.org/mala>.

Malawi 2015 Country Review. Country Report. CountryWatch Incorporated, July 2015.

"Reinventing Apprenticeship and Rites of Passage: An Entry into the Urban Economy in Sub-Saharan Africa." *World Bank IK Notes* 20 (2000). http://www.worldbank.org/afr/ik/iknt20.pdf.

"The Constitution of the Zambezi Evangelical Church – Malawi." Zambezi Evangelical Church, 2014.

"The First 50 Years of the Zambesi (Industrial) Mission 1890s–1940s Based on the Mission's Magazine." Zambesi Mission (Unpublished), 2009.

"The World Factbook." *CIA.* <https://www.cia.gov/library/publications /the-world-factbook/geos/mi.html>.

"World Population Prospects, the 2012 Revision," *United Nations.* <http://esa.un.org/wpp/Excel-Data/population.htm>, (accessed 12 June 2015).

Endnotes

[1] Paul Bowers, "Theological Education in Africa: Why Does It Matter?" *African Journal of Evangelical Theology*, 26:2 (2007), 149.

[2] F. Ross Kinsler (ed.), *Ministry by the People: Theological Education by Extension* (Geneva: WCC, 1983).

[3] Craig Ott and Gene Wilson, *Global Church Planting: Biblical Principles and Best Practices for Multiplication* (Grand Rapids: Baker, 2011), 69; Craig Ott, *Encountering Theology of Mission: Biblical Foundations, Historical Developments, and Contemporary Issues*, Encountering Mission (Grand Rapids: Baker Academic, 2010), xxv.

[4] Philip Jenkins, *The New Faces of Christianity: Believing the Bible in the Global South* (New York: Oxford University Press, 2006), 9; F. Ross Kinsler, "Theological Education by Extension: Equipping God's People for Ministry," in F. Ross Kinsler (ed.), *Ministry by the People: Theological Education by Extension* (Geneva: WCC, 1983), 2.

[5] Gideon Para-Mallam, "Theological Trends in Africa: Implications for Missions and Evangelism." *Lausanne Reports*, 03, 2008; Serah Wambua, "Mission Spirituality and Authentic Discipleship: An African Reflection," *Seoul Consultation, Study Commission IX* (Seoul; Edinburgh 2009, 2010), 46; Ralph D Winter, *Frontiers in Mission: Discovering and Surmounting Barriers to the Missio Dei* (Pasadena: William Carey International University Press, 2008), 31; Philip E. Morrison, "Implications of Paul's Model for Leadership Training in Light of Church Growth in Africa," *African Journal of Evangelical Theology* 30:1 (2011), 56; Paul Kisau, "The Key to the African Heart: Rethinking Missionary Strategy in Africa," *Africa Journal of Evangelical Theology* 17:2 (1998), 90.

[6] Emilio Castro, "Foreword," in F. Ross Kinsler (ed.), *Ministry by the People: Theological Education by Extension* (Geneva: WCC, 1983), x; "Malawi | Operation World," *Operation World*, <http://www.operationworld.org /mala>; R. J. G. Hovil, "The Advantages and Disadvantages of Different Models of Training," *Trust in Christ Consultation* (Bath, 2001), 2; Fred Holland, "TEXT Africa: Programming for Ministry through Theological Education by Extension," in F. Ross Kinsler (ed.), *Ministry by the People: Theological Education by Extension* (Geneva: WCC, 1983), 106; Patricia J. Harrison, "Forty Years On: The Evolution of Theology by Extension," *Evangelical Review of Theology* 28:4 (2004), 315; Kinsler, *Ministry by the People*, 5; Morrison, "Implications of Paul's Model," 55–56.

[7] Carlos Mesters, "Bible Study Centre for People's Pastoral Action (Brazil): The Use of the Bible among the People," in F. Ross Kinsler (ed.), *Ministry by the People: Theological Education by Extension* (Geneva: WCC, 1983), 90–91; Kinsler, *Ministry by the People*, 1983, 9; Keith B. Anderson and N. Kiranga Gatimu, "Diocese of Mt Kenya East (Anglican): Meeting Community Needs through Theological Education by Extension," in F. Ross Kinsler (ed.), *Ministry by the People: Theological Education by Extension* (Geneva: WCC, 1983), 149; Jonathan D. Groves, *Reading Romans at Ground Level: A Contemporary Rural African Perspective* (Carlisle: Langham Global Library, 2015), 7, 26-27; Paul Kohls, "A Look at Church Leadership in Africa," *Africa Journal of Evangelical Theology* 17:2 (1998), 108.

⁸ Kinsler, *Ministry by the People*, 23; Harrison, "Forty Years On," 315; Castro, *Ministry by the People*, x; Davidson Kamayaya Chifungo, "An Oral Hermeneutics: A Critical Evaluation," PhD, Stellenbosch University, 2013, 182; Hovil, "The Advantages and Disadvantages of Different Models of Training," 2; Groves, *Reading Romans at Ground Level*, 7, 26; Kinsler, *Ministry by the People*, 9; Holland, *Ministry by the People*, 103, 106; George Patterson, "Extension Bible Institute (Northern Honduras): Theological Education and Evangelism by Extension," in F. Ross Kinsler (ed.), *Ministry by the People: Theological Education by Extension* (Geneva: WCC, 1983), 52.

⁹ Morrison, "Implications of Paul's Model," 55; Bowers, "Theological Education in Africa: Why Does It Matter?" 141–142; Castro, *Ministry by the People*, x; Kenneth B. Mulholland and Kelly de Jacobs, "Presbyterian Seminary of Guatemala: A Modest Experiment Becomes a Model for Change," in F. Ross Kinsler (ed.) *Ministry by the People: Theological Education by Extension* (Geneva: WCC, 1983), 34–35.

¹⁰ Castro, *Ministry by the People*; F. Ross Kinsler, "Preface," in F. Ross Kinsler (ed.), *Ministry by the People: Theological Education by Extension* (Geneva: WCC, 1983), xiii-xvi; Harrison, "Forty Years On."

¹¹ Hovil, "The Advantages and Disadvantages of Different Models of Training," 2.

¹² Earle Cairns, *Preach the Word!* (Maitland: Xulon Press, 2005), 23; Kenton C Anderson, *Choosing to Preach: A Comprehensive Introduction to Sermon Options and Structures* (Grand Rapids: Zondervan, 2006), Kindle Loc 2736; Thomas G. Long, "A New Focus for Teaching Preaching," in Thomas G. Long and Leonora Tubbs Tisdale (eds.), *Teaching Preaching as a Christian Practice: A New Approach to Homiletic Pedagogy* (Louisville, KY: Westminster John Knox Press, 2008), 3; Dawn Ottoni Wilhelm, "New Hermeneutic, Hew Homiletic, and New Directions: An US-North American Perspective," *Homiletic (Online)* 35:1 (2010), 19; Robert Stephen Reid, "Postmodernism and the Function of the New Homiletic in Post-Christendom Congregations," *Homiletic* 20:2 (1995), 7.

¹³ Steve Smith, *T4T: A Discipleship Re-Revolution* (Monument, CO: WIGTake Resources, 2011); Project Worldreach, *Train and Multiply*, <http://www.trainandmultiply.com/>; One Mission Society, "Village Church Planting," *Into Africa Project*, <http://www.intoafricaproject.org/vcp/index.html>.

¹⁴ John Swinton and Harriet Mowatt, *Practical Theology and Qualitative Research Methods* (London: SCM Press, 2006), Kindle Loc 92, 108, 559–596, 1755; John Ballard and Paul Pritchard, *Practical Theology in Action: Christian Thinking in the Service of Church and Society* (London: SPCK, 2006, 60–77).

¹⁵ Hovil, "The Advantages and Disadvantages of Different Models of Training," 1; Isaac Zokoue, "Educating for Servant Leadership in Africa," *Africa Journal of Evangelical Theology* 9:1 (1990), 11.

¹⁶ The statement by Barth is quoted in Eben K. Nhiwatiwa, *Preaching in the African Context: Why We Preach* (Nashville, TN: Langham, 2012), 25.

[17] Anderson, *Choosing to Preach*, 30; W. E. Sangster, *The Craft of the Sermon* (London: Epworth, 1954), 11; Haddon W Robinson, *Expository Preaching: Principles & Practice* (Leicester: Inter-Varsity, 2001), 15; Dennis M. Cahill, *The Shape of Preaching: Theory and Practice in Sermon Design* (Grand Rapids: Baker, 2007), 18; Howard Williams, *My Word* (Norwich: SCM, 1973), 1–7; David Martyn Lloyd-Jones, *Preaching and Preachers* (London: Hodder and Stoughton, 1971), 9.

[18] John R. W. Stott, *I Believe in Preaching* (London: Hodder and Stoughton, 1982), 51; Fred B. Craddock, *As One Without Authority: Fourth Edition Revised and with New Sermons* (Atlanta: Chalice, 2001), 9, 14; D. A Carson and Timothy J Keller, *Gospel-Centered Ministry* (Wheaton: Crossway, 2011), 8–9; Stott, *I Believe in Preaching*, 71, 73, 75; David Day, "Six Feet Above Contradiction? An Overview," in David Day, Jeff Astley, Leslie J. Francis (eds.), *A Reader On Preaching: Making Connections* (Aldershot: Ashgate, 2005), 5; Christopher Ash, *The Priority of Preaching* (Fearn: Christian Focus, 2009), 19.

[19] Ash, *The Priority of Preaching*, 17; Lloyd-Jones, *Preaching and Preachers*, 9–25; "Editorial: Empty Hearts and Empty Minds," *Africa Journal of Evangelical Theology* 117:2 (1998), 83–84.

[20] Ash, *The Priority of Preaching*, 15–16; Derek J. Prime and Alistair Begg, *On Being A Pastor: Understanding Our Calling and Work* (Chicago, IL: Moody, 2004), 177; Stott, *I Believe in Preaching*, 16, 17.

[21] Ash, *The Priority of Preaching*, 27.

[22] Chifungo, "An Oral Hermeneutics," 112.

[23] J. A. Motyer, *Preaching?: Simple Teaching on Simply Preaching* (Fearn: Christian Focus, 2013), 89; Bryan Chapell, *Christ-Centered Preaching: Redeeming the Expository Sermon*, 2nd ed. (Grand Rapids: Baker Academic, 2005), 35; Tim Hawkins, *Messages That Move* (Epsom: The Good Book Company, 2013), 24; Thomas G. Long, "The Distance We Have Travelled: Changing Trends in Preaching," in David Day, Jeff Astley, and Leslie J. Francis (eds.), *A Reader On Preaching: Making Connections* (Aldershot: Ashgate, 2005), 12; Robinson, *Expository Preaching*, 3, 5, 13, 23; Cairns, *Preach the Word!*, 23; Stephen F. Olford and David L. Olford, *Anointed Expository Preaching* (Nashville, TN: B&H, 1998), 69; Sangster, *The Craft of the Sermon*, 31; Simon Vibert, *Excellence in Preaching: Learning from the Best* (Nottingham: Inter-Varsity Press, 2011), 13; Ash, *The Priority of Preaching*, 108; Thomas G. Long, *The Witness of Preaching*, 2nd ed. (Louisville, KY: Westminster John Knox, 2005), 52; Haddon W. Robinson, *Biblical Preaching: The Development and Delivery of Expository Messages* (Grand Rapids: Baker Academic, 2001), 20–29.

[24] Cairns, *Preach the Word!*, 16–19; Robinson, *Biblical Preaching*, 17–18; Robert A. Allen, "The Expository Sermon: Cultural or Biblical," *Journal of Ministry and Theology* 2:2 (1998), 212–214.

[25] Allen, "The Expository Sermon: Cultural or Biblical," 214–216; Cairns, *Preach the Word!*, 23; Long, "Teaching Preaching as a Christian Practice," 3; Wilhelm, "New Hermeneutic, Hew Homiletic, and New Directions," 19; Reid, "Postmodernism and the Function of the New Homiletic in Post-Christendom Congregations," 7;

Craddock, *As One Without Authority*; W. E Sangster, *The Craft of Sermon Construction* (London: Pickering and Inglis, 1978); Eugene L. Lowry, "The Revolution of Sermonic Shape," in Gail R. O' Day and Thomas G. Long (eds.), *Listening to the Word: Studies in Honor of Fred B. Craddock* (Nashville, TN: Abingdon, 1993), 93–112; Eugene L. Lowry, *How to Preach a Parable: Designs for Narrative Sermons* (Nashville, TN: Abingdon, 1989); Eugene L. Lowry, *Homiletical Plot: The Sermon as Narrative Art Form*, Expanded Edition (Louisville, KY: Westminster John Knox, 2000); Long, "The Distance We Have Travelled: Changing Trends in Preaching," 11–16.

[26] Anderson, *Choosing to Preach*.

[27] Myles MacBean, "The Homiletic Window: A Model for Reflective Preaching Praxis," *Evangelical Review of Theology*, 41:3 (2017), 209–221; Thomas G. Long, *The Witness of Preaching*, 2nd ed. (Louisville, KY: Westminster John Knox, 2005); Kenton C. Anderson, *Choosing to Preach: A Comprehensive Introduction to Sermon Options and Structures*.

[28] Hovil, "The Advantages and Disadvantages of Different Models of Training," 1.

[29] Hovil, "The Advantages and Disadvantages of Different Models of Training," 12–18.

[30] Patterson, *Ministry by the People*, 60; Michael David Sills, "Training Leaders for the Majority World Church in the 21st Century," *Global Missiology English* 3:1 (2004), 175; Russell W. West, "Church-Based Theological Education: When the Seminary Goes back to Church," *Journal of Religious Leadership* 2:2 (2003), 113–165.

[31] Bunting, Ian D., *The Place to Train. A Report on Theological Training for the Urban Churches of Britain*, A report produced for the Kingham Trust. Unpublished, 1989, 41, quoted in Hovil, "The Advantages and Disadvantages of Different Models of Training," 12.

[32] Hovil, "The Advantages and Disadvantages of Different Models of Training," 18.

[33] Hovil, "The Advantages and Disadvantages of Different Models of Training," 12, 18; Patterson, *Ministry by the People*, 60.

[34] Hovil, "The Advantages and Disadvantages of Different Models of Training," 12; Sam Westman Burton, *Disciple Mentoring: Theological Education by Extension* (Pasadena, CA: William Carey Library, 2000), 4, 18; R. Jeremy G. Hovil, "Transforming Theological Education in the Church of the Province of Uganda (Anglican)," D.Th, University of Stellenbosch, 2005; R. Jeremy G. Hovil, "An Investigation into Alternative and Appropriate Models of Theological Education for Non-Western Contexts," *MTh Dissertation*, Spurgeon's College (University of Wales), 1999, 3; Mark Young, "What Forms of Theological Education are Appropriate for Post-Communist Europe?" A Paper Delivered at the Consultation on Theological Education and Leadership Development in Post-Communist Europe (Oradea, Romania, October 4–8th, 1994), *Transformation* 16:1 (1999), 8, quoted in Hovil, "The Advantages and Disadvantages of Different Models of Training," 3.

[35] "Malawi: Operation World;" "World Population Prospects, the 2012 Revision," *United Nations*, <http://esa.un.org/wpp/Excel-Data/population.htm>.

[36] B. R. Rafael, *A Short History of Malawi* (Limbe: Popular Publications, 1988); John McCracken, *A History of Malawi: 1859–1966* (Woodbridge: Boydell & Brewer Ltd, 2012); John G. Pike, "A Pre-Colonial History of Malawi," *The Nyasaland Journal* 18:1 (1965), 22–54; Owen J. M. Kalinga, *Historical Dictionary of Malawi* (Lanham: Rowman & Littlefield, 2012).

[37] "Malawi | Data," World Bank, <http://data.worldbank.org/country/ Malawi>; "The World Factbook," CIA, <https://www.cia.gov/library/ publications/the-world-factbook/geos/mi.html>; "Human Development Index and Its Components | Human Development Reports," United Nations Development Programme, <http://hdr.undp.org/en/content/table-1-human-development-index-and-its-components>; *Malawi 2015 Country Review*, Country Report, Country Watch Incorporated, July 2015; *Country Reports: Malawi*, Country Report, IHS Global Inc., 2015.

[38] "Malawi: Operation World;" "Country – Malawi," *Joshua Project*, <http://joshuaproject.net/countries/MI>; "The World Factbook," CIA, <https://www.cia.gov/library/publications/the-world-factbook/geos/mi.html>.

[39] Patrick Johnstone and Jason Mandryk, *Operation World: 21st Century Edition* (Milton Keynes: Paternoster Press, 2001).

[40] "The First 50 Years of the Zambesi (Industrial) Mission 1890s–1940s Based on the Mission's Magazine," Zambesi Mission, Unpublished, 2009, 2; Kelvin N. Banda, *A Brief History of Education in Malaŵi* (Blantyre: Dzuka, 1982), 11, 13; McCracken, *A History of Malawi, 1859–1966*, 107; Pike, "A Pre-Colonial History of Malawi," 1; Kalinga, *Historical Dictionary of Malawi*, 485; D. D. Phiri, *History of Malawi: From Earliest Times to the Year 1915* (Blantyre: CLAIM, 2004), 152; Gordon W. Smith, Bridglal Pachai, and Roger K. Tangri, *Malawi Past and Present: Selected Papers from the University of Malawi History Conference* (Blantyre: CLAIM, 1971), 71, 134; Bridglal Pachai, *Malawi; the History of the Nation* (Harlow: Longman, 1973), 40, 88, 133; Fiedler, *The Story of Faith Missions*, 28, 53, 69, 80, 82, 207; Christoff Martin Pauw, *The History of the Nkhoma Synod of the Church of Central Africa, Presbyterian, 1889–1962* (Lusaka: Church of Central Africa Presbyterian, 1962), 30–33.

[41] Klaus Fiedler, *The Story of Faith Missions* (Oxford: Regnum, 1994), 82.

[42] Johnstone and Mandryk, *Operation World: 21st Century Edition*, 552.

[43] "The Constitution of the Zambezi Evangelical Church – Malawi," Zambezi Evangelical Church, 2014.

[44] John K. Marah, "The Virtues and Challenges in Traditional African Education," *The Journal of Pan African Studies* 1:4 (2006), 17; Ernst Wendland and Salimo Hachibamba, *Galu Wamkota: Missiological Reflections from South – Central Africa* (Zomba: Kachere Series, 2007), 275; J. W. M. van Breugel, *Chewa Traditional Religion* (Blantyre: CLAIM, 2001), 265, 266; J. C. Chakanza, *Initiation Rites for Boys in Lomwe Society in Malawi and Other Essays* (Zomba: Kachere Series, 2005), 12, 19, 31; David G. Scanlon, "Conflicting Traditions in African Education," in David G. Scanlon (ed.), *Traditions of African Education* (New York: Columbia University, 1964), 4; Jean-Marie Hyacinthe Quenum, "Growing up and Maturing in African Perspective," *Academia*, n.d., 4, 7,

<https://www.academia.edu/1533345/Growing_up_and_Maturing_in_African_Perspective>; "Reinventing Apprenticeship and Rites of Passage: An Entry into the Urban Economy in Sub-Saharan Africa," *World Bank IK Notes* 20, (2000), http://www.worldbank.org/afr/ik/iknt20.pdf; .

[45] Scanlon, "Conflicting Traditions in African Education," 4.

[46] James A. Anderson, "Cognitive Style and Multicultural Populations," *Journal of Teacher Education* 39:1 (1988), 4, 6, 7; Glaucoma De Vita, "Learning Styles, Culture and Inclusive Instruction in the Multicultural Classroom: A Business and Management Perspective," *Innovations in Education and Teaching International* 38:2 (2001), 167; Dorothy N. Bowen and Earle A. Bowen, "Contextualisation of Teaching Methodology in Theological Education," *Conference of Theological Educators*, Limuru, Kenya, 1988, 5.

[47] Pat Guild, "The Culture/Learning Style Connection," *Educating for Diversity* 51:8 (1994), 16–21.

[48] Simy Joy and David A. Kolb, "Are There Cultural Differences in Learning Style?" *International Journal of Intercultural Relations* 1:33 (2009), 69–85.

[49] Frank Coffield et al., *Learning Styles and Pedagogy in Post-16 Learning: A Systematic and Critical Review* (London: The Learning and Skills Research Centre, 2004), 138–143; Alice Y. Kolb and David A. Kolb, *The Kolb Learning Style Inventory – Version 3.1: 2005* (Boston; London: Hay Resources Direct, 2005); Jim Caple and Paul Martin, "Reflections of Two Pragmatists: A Critique of Honey and Mumford's Learning Styles," *Industrial and Commercial Training*, 26:1 (1994), 16–20.

[50] Chris Howles, "African Learning-Style," *BA Dissertation for "Theology and World Mission,"* Oak Hill Theological College (University of Middlesex), 2010; Peter Honey and Alan Mumford, *The Learning Styles Helper's Guide* (Maidenhead: Peter Honey, 2000); Peter Honey, *The Learning Styles Questionnaire* (London: Pearson Clinical and Talent Assessment, 2006).

[51] Kolb, David A., *Experiential Learning: Experience as the Source of Learning and Development* (Englewood Cliffs: Prentice Hall, 1984).

[52] Honey, *The Learning Styles Questionnaire*.

[53] Eben K. Nhiwatiwa, *Preaching in the African Context: How We Preach*, (Nashville, TN: Langham, 2012), 7; Chifungo, "An Oral Hermeneutics;" Nhiwatiwa, *Why We Preach*; Groves, *Reading Romans at Ground Level*; "Homiletics and Preaching in Africa," in William H. Willimon and Richard Lischer (eds.), *Concise Encyclopaedia of Preaching* (Louisville, KY: Westminster John Knox, 1995), 229–231.

[54] Nhiwatiwa, *How We Preach*, 20–21; Nhiwatiwa, *Why We Preach*, 83–84; Chifungo, "An Oral Hermeneutics," 131.

[55] Groves, *Reading Romans at Ground Level*, 7; Nhiwatiwa, *Why We Preach*, 80.

[56] Nhiwatiwa, *How We Preach*, 12,13; Chifungo, "An Oral Hermeneutics," 83.

[57] Groves, *Reading Romans at Ground Level*, 12, 76; Nhiwatiwa, *How We Preach*, 18; Nhiwatiwa, *Why We Preach*, 80; Chifungo, "An Oral Hermeneutics," 133; Conrad Mbewe, *Pastoral Preaching: Building a People for God* (Carlisle: Langham, 2006).

[58] Groves, *Reading Romans at Ground Level*, 76; Nhiwatiwa, *How We Preach*, 32.
[59] Chifungo, "An Oral Hermeneutics," 82.
[60] Chifungo, "An Oral Hermeneutics," 131.
[61] Nhiwatiwa, *How We Preach*, 25, 67; Chifungo, "An Oral Hermeneutics," 159, 170; Conrad Mbewe, *Pastoral Preaching: Building a People for God* (Carlisle: Langham, 2017).
[62] Nhiwatiwa, *How We Preach*, 25–26, 71, 84; Chifungo, "An Oral Hermeneutics," 83, 84, 162–171; "Homiletics and Preaching in Africa," in William H. Willimon and Richard Lischer, eds., *Concise Encyclopaedia of Preaching* (Louisville, KY: Westminster John Knox, 1995), 229–231.
[63] Harrison, "Forty Years On," 315; Herbert M. Zorn, *Viability in Context: A Study of the Financial Viability of Theological Education in the Third World – Seedbed or Sheltered Garden?* (Bromley: WCC, 1973); Holland, *Ministry by the People*, 103–105.
[64] Holland, *Ministry by the People*, 106; Kinsler, *Ministry by the People*, xv; Ralph D. Winter, "The Largest Stumbling Block to Leadership Development in the Global Church," *International Journal of Frontier Missions* 20:3 (2003), 88.
[65] Patterson, *Ministry by the People*, 52; Holland, *Ministry by the People*, 109; Kinsler, *Ministry by the People*, 1983, 1.
[66] Kinsler, *Ministry by the People*, 1983, 9; Leslie Newbigin, "Theological Education in a World Perspective," *Churchman* 93:2 (1979), 113.
[67] Kinsler, *Ministry by the People*, 1983, xiii–xiv; Richard Sales and Jacob Liphok, "Grassroots Theology in Botswana," in F. Ross Kinsler *(ed.)*, *Ministry by the People: Theological Education by Extension* (Geneva: WCC, 1983), 140–141; Holland, *Ministry by the People*, 105–106; Hovil, "The Advantages and Disadvantages of Different Models of Training," 19.
[68] Zorn, *Viability in Context: A Study of the Financial Viability of Theological Education in the Third World – Seedbed or Sheltered Garden?*; Ross Kinsler, "Doing Ministry for a Change: Theological Education for the Twenty-First Century," *Ministerial Formation* 108 (2007), 11; Hovil, "The Advantages and Disadvantages of Different Models of Training," 20–21; Kinsler, *Ministry by the People* (1983), 23; Mulholland and de Jacobs, *Ministry by the People*, 40.
[69] Patterson, *Ministry by the People*, 57; Holland, *Ministry by the People*, 107.
[70] Agustin Batlle and Rosario Batlle, "Theological Community of Chile: Extension Training for Indigenous Church Leaders," in F. Ross Kinsler (ed.), *Ministry by the People: Theological Education by Extension* (Geneva: WCC, 1983), 66; Castro, *Ministry by the People*, ix; Bumija Mshana and Dean Paterson, "Lutheran synod and Roman Catholic diocese of Arusha: Training Village Ministries in Tanzania," in F. Ross Kinsler (ed.), *Ministry by the People: Theological Education by Extension* (Geneva: WCC, 1983), 127; Kinsler, *Ministry by the People*, 1983, xv; Kinsler, *Ministry by the People*, 1983, 6, 11, 22; Patterson, *Ministry by the People*, 56; Mulholland and de Jacobs, *Ministry by the People*, 10.
[71] Kinsler, "Doing Ministry for a Change," 12; Harrison, "Forty Years On."
[72] Harrison, "Forty Years On," 323–328; Hovil, "The Advantages and Disadvantages of Different Models of Training," 21–24.

[73] Mulholland and de Jacobs, *Ministry by the People*, 40; Patterson, *Ministry by the People*, 53; Michael Crowley, "Passing on the Faith," in F. Ross Kinsler (ed.), *Ministry by the People: Theological Education by Extension* (Geneva: WCC, 1983), 43; Holland, *Ministry by the People*, 113–114.

[74] Holland, *Ministry by the People*, 107.

[75] Holland, *Ministry by the People*, 105–106; Hovil, "The Advantages and Disadvantages of Different Models of Training," 24; Harrison, "Forty Years On," 323–328.

[76] Kinsler, "Doing Ministry for a Change," 10; Hovil, "The Advantages and Disadvantages of Different Models of Training," 34–36; Hovil, "Transforming Theological Education," 307–342; Phillip Turley, "Extending the Fence: Suggestions for the Future of TEE in Africa," *Africa Journal of Evangelical Theology* 10:1 (1991), 40.

[77] Kinsler, "Doing Ministry for a Change," 13.

[78] Hovil, "An Investigation into Alternative and Appropriate Models of Theological Education for Non-Western Contexts;" Hovil, "Transforming Theological Education;" R. J. G. Hovil, A. E. Carl, and H. J. Hendriks, "The Promise of Dynamic Curriculum Development Models for Transforming Multi-Level Systems of Theological Education: A Ugandan Case Study," *Dutch Reformed Theological Journal* 47:3&4 (2006), 534–546; Hovil, "The Advantages and Disadvantages of Different Models of Training."

[79] Hovil, "The Advantages and Disadvantages of Different Models of Training," 3–5; Mark Young, "What Forms of Theological Education Are Appropriate for Post-Communist Europe?" A Paper Consultation on Theological Education and Leadership Development in Post-Communist Europe (Oradea, Romania, October 4–8th, 1994).

[80] Young, "What Forms of Theological Education Are Appropriate for Post-Communist Europe?" 8.

[81] Orlando E. Costas, "Theological Education and Mission," in C. Rene Padilla (ed.) *New Alternatives in Theological Education* (Oxford: Regnum, 1988), 8; Hovil, "The Advantages and Disadvantages of Different Models of Training," 6.

[82] Hovil, "The Advantages and Disadvantages of Different Models of Training," 6–11.

[83] Harrison, "Forty Years On," 323-326; Hovil, "The Advantages and Disadvantages of Different Models of Training," 7–8; Tite Tienou, "Contextualisation of Theology for Theological Education," in Paul Bowers (ed.) *Evangelical Theological Education Today: 2. An Agenda for Renewal* (Nairobi: Evangel Publishing House, 1982), 42–52; Darren Cronshaw, "Re-envisioning Theological Education, Mission and the Local Church," *Mission Studies*, 28 (2011), 91–115.

[84] Nhiwatiwa, *How We Preach*, 29–52; Nhiwatiwa, *Why We Preach*, 33–40; Hovil, "The Advantages and Disadvantages of Different Models of Training," 7; Tokunboh Adeyemo (ed.), *Africa Bible Commentary* (Grand Rapids: Zondervan, 2010), 3–4; Delta Kapteina, "The Formation of African Evangelical Theology," *Africa Journal of Evangelical Theology* 25:1 (2006), 78–79.

Bibliography and Endnotes

[85] Chifungo, "An Oral Hermeneutics;" Harrison, "Forty Years On," 322; Nhiwatiwa, *How We Preach*, 20–24; Groves, *Reading Romans at Ground Level*, 7–9.

[86] Chifungo, "An Oral Hermeneutics;" Nhiwatiwa, *How We Preach*, 53–89; Nhiwatiwa, *Why We Preach*, 50–55.

[87] Harrison, "Forty Years On," 326–327; Nhiwatiwa, *How We Preach*, 91–106; Hovil, "The Advantages and Disadvantages of Different Models of Training," 8; Sills, "Training Leaders for the Majority World Church in the 21st Century," 176.

[88] Hovil, "The Advantages and Disadvantages of Different Models of Training," 31; Harrison, "Forty Years On," 316.

[89] Harrison, "Forty Years On," 316, 321; Hovil, "The Advantages and Disadvantages of Different Models of Training," 9.

[90] Hovil, "The Advantages and Disadvantages of Different Models of Training," 9.

[91] Harrison, "Forty Years On," 320; Hovil, "The Advantages and Disadvantages of Different Models of Training," 8; Robert W. Ferris, "The Future of Theological Education," in Robert L. Youngblood (ed.), *Cyprus: TEE Come of Age* (Exeter: Paternoster, 1986), 57.

[92] Hovil, "The Advantages and Disadvantages of Different Models of Training," 7.

[93] Harrison, "Forty Years On," 321; Patterson, *Ministry by the People*, 57; Holland, *Ministry by the People*, 107; Hovil, "The Advantages and Disadvantages of Different Models of Training," 29.

[94] Andy Hobson, "Mentoring and Coaching for New Leaders: Summary Report," National College for School Leadership, 2003, 5–6; Jackie Arnold, *Coaching Skills for Leaders in the Workplace: How to Develop, Motivate and Get the Best from Your Staff* (Oxford: How to Books, 2010), xiii.

[95] Hovil, "The Advantages and Disadvantages of Different Models of Training," 7, 25; Gary R. Collins, *Christian Coaching: Helping Others Turn Potential into Reality* (Colorado Springs, CO: NavPress, 2001), 235–248; Steven L. Ogne, *TransforMissional Coaching: Empowering Spiritual Leaders in a Changing Ministry World* (Nashville, TN: B&H, 2008), 79–81; Jane Creswell, *Christ-Centered Coaching: 7 Benefits for Ministry Leaders* (Atlanta: Chalice, 2006); Linda J. Miller and Chad W. Hall, *Coaching for Christian Leaders: A Practical Guide* (Atlanta: Chalice, 2007); Tony Stoltzfus, *Leadership Coaching: The Disciplines, Skills and Heart of a Christian Coach* (Virginia Beach, VA: Coach22, 2005); Shane Parker, "The Supervisor as Mentor-Coach in Theological Field Education," *Christian Education Journal*, 6:1 (2009), 51–63.

[96] Carol Wilson, *Best Practice in Performance Coaching: A Handbook for Leaders, Coaches, HR Professionals and Organizations*, 1st Edition (Kogan Page, 2011), 7, 15; Hobson, "Mentoring and Coaching for New Leaders," 2; Stoltzfus, *Leadership Coaching*, 5–30.

[97] James M. Hunt and Joseph R. Weintraub, *The Coaching Organization: A Strategy for Developing Leaders* (London: Sage, 2006), 6; Hobson, "Mentoring and Coaching for New Leaders," 6–7; Daniel Harkavy, *Becoming a Coaching Leader: The Proven Strategy for Building a Team of Champions* (Nashville, TN: Nelson Business, 2007), 4.

[98] Arnold, *Coaching Skills for Leaders in the Workplace*, 28; Hobson, "Mentoring and Coaching for New Leaders," 20; Wilson, *Best Practice in Performance Coaching*, 15; Collins, *Christian Coaching*, 19.

[99] Hobson, "Mentoring and Coaching for New Leaders," 20; Myles Downey, *Effective Coaching: Lessons from the Coaches' Coach*, 2nd ed. (New York; London: Texere, 2003), 9, 200; Wilson, *Best Practice in Performance Coaching*, 8; Collins, *Christian Coaching*, 16; Arnold, *Coaching Skills for Leaders in the Workplace*, 16.

[100] Wilson, *Best Practice in Performance Coaching*, 20–49, 45–54; Ogne, *TransforMissional Coaching*, 101–120.

[101] Hunt and Weintraub, *The Coaching Organization*, 6, 202; Arnold, *Coaching Skills for Leaders in the Workplace*, 239; Ogne, *TransforMissional Coaching*, 69–81.

[102] Hunt and Weintraub, *The Coaching Organization*, 195; Collins, *Christian Coaching*, 45; Hobson, "Mentoring and Coaching for New Leaders," 18; Wilson, *Best Practice in Performance Coaching*, 98.

[103] Hunt and Weintraub, *The Coaching Organization*, 57–64.

[104] Stephen Taylor, "An Introduction," in *Franchising Hospitality Services*, ed. Conrad Lashley and Alison J. Morrison, The Hospitality, Leisure and Tourism Series (Oxford; Boston: Butterworth/Heinemann, 2000), 4.

[105] Taylor, "An Introduction," 7–11; Shane Scott and Chester Spell, "Factors for New Franchise Success," *Sloan Management Review* 39:3 (1998), 44; Christina Fulop, "History and Development," in Conrad Lashley and Alison J. Morrison (eds.), *Franchising Hospitality Services*, The Hospitality, Leisure and Tourism Series (Oxford: Butterworth, 2000), 26.

[106] Fulop, "History and Development," 22, 31; Bradley J. Sugars and Brad Sugars, *Successful Franchising: Expert Advice on Buying, Selling and Creating Winning Franchises*, 1st ed. (New York: McGraw-Hill, 2006), 6; Taylor, "An Introduction," 3; Iain Maitland, *Franchising: A Practical Guide for Franchisors and Franchisees* (Winnipeg, MB: Mercury, 1991), 22–26, 73; Alison J. Morrison, "Entrepreneurs or Intrapreneurs?," in Conrad Lashley and Alison J. Morrison (eds.), *Franchising Hospitality Services*, The Hospitality, Leisure and Tourism Series (Oxford; Boston: Butterworth/Heinemann, 2000), 68; Clive Sawyer, *How to Franchise Your Business: The Plain Speaking Guide for Business Owners* (London: Live It Publishing, 2011), 59–62, 220; Stewart Germann, "Franchise Right," *Chartered Accountants Journal*, 2009, 72–73; David A. Light, "Franchising," *Harvard Business Review* 75:3 (1997), 15.

[107] Scott and Spell, "Factors for New Franchise Success," 44, 47–48; Sawyer, *How to Franchise Your Business*, 223–4; Maitland, *Franchising*, 24–26; Conrad Lashley, "Empowered Franchisees?" in Conrad Lashley and Alison J. Morrison (ed.), *Franchising Hospitality Services*, The Hospitality, Leisure and Tourism Series (Oxford; Boston: Butterworth/Heinemann, 2000), 92; Light, "Franchising," 15.

[108] Maitland, *Franchising*, 11; Germann, "Franchise Right," 73.

[109] Smith, *T4T*; Project Worldreach, *Train & Multiply*; One Mission Society, "Village Church Planting."

[110] John Patrick O'Connor, *Reproducible Pastoral Training: Church Planting Guidelines from the Teachings of George Patterson* (Pasadena: William Carey Library, 2006), 169; Smith, *T4T*, 23.

[111] O'Connor, *Reproducible Pastoral Training*, 68.

[112] George Patterson, "Foreword," in John Patrick O'Connor, *Reproducible Pastoral Training: Church Planting Guidelines from the Teachings of George Patterson* (Pasadena: William Carey Library, 2006), xv-xvi; O'Connor, *Reproducible Pastoral Training*, 1, 16, 20; Ott and Wilson, *Global Church Planting*, x, 72; Smith, *T4T*, 38.

[113] O'Connor, *Reproducible Pastoral Training*, 2.

[114] O'Connor, *Reproducible Pastoral Training*, 173; Ott and Wilson, *Global Church Planting*, 61, 70–71, 100; Tom A. Steffen, *The Facilitator Era: Beyond Pioneer Church Multiplication* (Eugene, OR: Wipf and Stock, 2011).

[115] O'Connor, *Reproducible Pastoral Training*, 9, 67.

[116] O'Connor, *Reproducible Pastoral Training*, 66–67, 133; Ott and Wilson, *Global Church Planting*, 73.

[117] O'Connor, *Reproducible Pastoral Training*, 15–16, 173, 306; Ott and Wilson, *Global Church Planting*, 73, 86, 108–12, 193; Hovil, "The Advantages and Disadvantages of Different Models of Training," 8; Robert J Vajko, "The Transformation of Society by Planting New Churches," *Ogbomoso Journal of Theology* 16:3 (2011), 108–112; Smith, *T4T*.

[118] Bowers, "Theological Education in Africa: Why Does It Matter?" 149; Smith, *T4T*, 22.

[119] Patterson, *Ministry by the People*, 52-60; Sills, "Training Leaders for the Majority World Church in the 21st Century," 178.

[120] Gary Thomas, *How To Do Your Research Project: A Guide for Students in Education and Applied Social Sciences*, 2nd ed. (Thousand Oaks, CA: Sage, 2013), 126; Colin Robson, *How to Do a Research Project: A Guide for Undergraduate Students*, 1st ed. (Malden: John Wiley & Sons, 2007), 21–23.

[121] Thomas, *How To Do Your Research Project*, 119–124; Nicholas Walliman, *Your Research Project: A Step-by-Step Guide for the First-Time Researcher*, 2nd ed. (London: Sage, 2005), 20–21.

[122] Thomas, *How To Do Your Research Project*, 105; Swinton and Mowatt, *Practical Theology*, Kindle Loc 776, 3063.

[123] D. A. Carson, *The Gagging of God: Christianity Confronts Pluralism* (Grand Rapids: Zondervan, 2002), 121; Martyn Denscombe, *Ground Rules For Social Research: Guidelines for Good Practice* (Maidenhead: McGraw-Hill International, 2009), 143.

[124] Swinton and Mowatt, *Practical Theology*, Kindle Loc 825–887, 1026, 3063; Denscombe, *Ground Rules For Social Research*, 131–135; Mark J. Cartledge, *Practical Theology: Charismatic and Empirical Perspectives* (Eugene, OR: Wipf & Stock, 2012), 69–76; Colin Robson, *How to Do a Research Project*, 21; Norman K. Denzin and Yvonna S. Lincoln, "Introduction: The Discipline and Practice of Qualitative Research," in Norman K. Denzin and Yvonna S. Lincoln (eds.),*The SAGE Handbook of Qualitative Research* (London: Sage, 2011), 1–20; Thomas, *How To Do Your Research Project*, 126; Norman K. Denzin, *The Research Act: A Theoretical Introduction to Sociological Methods* (Chicago, IL: Aldine, 1970), 26.

[125] Thomas, *How To Do Your Research Project*, 145–146, 183; Swinton and Mowatt, *Practical Theology*, Kindle Loc 1023, 1025, 3063, 3939; Norman K. Denzin and Yvonna S. Lincoln, *The SAGE Handbook of Qualitative Research*, London: SAGE, 2011, 5, 665; Creswell, John W., *Research Design: Qualitative, Quantitative, and Mixed Method Approaches*. 2nd ed. (Thousand Oaks, CA: Sage, 2003), 3-4, 17, 19; Martyn Denscombe, *The Good Research Guide*, Maidenhead: McGraw-Hill International, 2007, 107–121; John W. Creswell, "Controversies in Mixed Methods Research," in Norman K. Denzin and Yvonna S. Lincoln (eds.), *The SAGE Handbook of Qualitative Research* (London: Sage, 2011), 269–284; Charles Teddle and Abbas Tashakkori, "Mixed Methods Research," in Norman K. Denzin and Yvonna S. Lincoln (eds.), *The SAGE Handbook of Qualitative Research* (London: Sage, 2006), 285–300.

[126] Thomas, *How To Do Your Research Project*, 150–155; Judith Bell, *Doing Your Research Project: A Guide for First-time Researchers in Education, Health and Social Science* (Maidenhead: McGraw-Hill Education, 2010), 8–10; Robson, *How to Do a Research Project*, 26–28; Denscombe, *The Good Research Guide*, 35–47.

[127] Thomas, *How To Do Your Research Project*, 170–181, Creswell, *Research Design*, 13.

[128] Thomas, *How To Do Your Research Project*, 173–176.

[129] Thomas, *How To Do Your Research Project*, 41–42.

[130] Thomas, *How To Do Your Research Project*, 42.

[131] Thomas, *How To Do Your Research Project*, 176; Cartledge, *Practical Theology*, 74–75; Johannes A. van der Ven, "An Empirical or a Normative Approach to Practical-Theological Research? A False Dilemma," *Journal of Empirical Theology*, 15:2 (2002), 16; Bell, *Doing Your Research Project*, 11–12; Robson, *How to Do a Research Project*, 41–44; Denscombe, *The Good Research Guide*, 7–34.

[132] Walliman, *Your Research Project*, 314; Thomas, *How To Do Your Research Project*, 145–146; Swinton and Mowatt, *Practical Theology*, Kindle Loc 3063; Denzin and Lincoln, *The SAGE Handbook of Qualitative Research*, 5; Denzin, *The Research Act*, 310; Denscombe, *The Good Research Guide*, 173–205.

[133] Thomas, *How To Do Your Research Project*, 194–199; Cartledge, *Practical Theology*, 71–72; Denscombe, *The Good Research Guide*, 173–205.

[134] Thomas, *How To Do Your Research Project*, 198; Bell, *Doing Your Research Project*, 161–162; Robson, *How to Do a Research Project*, 74–75.

[135] See Appendix A.

[136] See Appendix A.

[137] Thomas, *How To Do Your Research Project*, 212, 214; Bell, *Doing Your Research Project*, 141–142; Denscombe, *The Good Research Guide*, 153–172.

[138] Cartledge, *Practical Theology*, 73; Denscombe, *The Good Research Guide*, 227–246; Thomas, *How To Do Your Research Project*, 204–206, 239–242.

[139] Howles, "African Learning-Style;" Honey, *The Learning Styles Questionnaire*.

[140] Thomas, *How To Do Your Research Project*, 132–136; Robson, *Real World Research: A Resource for Social Scientists and Practitioner-Researchers*, 2nd ed. (Oxford: John Wiley & Sons, 2002), 157, 262.

[141] Robson, *Real World Research*, 161–162; Thomas, *How To Do Your Research Project*, 135–136.

[142] Thomas, *How To Do Your Research Project*, 136; Robson, *Real World Research*, 157.

[143] Thomas, *How To Do Your Research Project*, 235, 236, 239–242; Juliet M. Corbin and Anselm Strauss, *Basics of Qualitative Research: Techniques and Procedures for Developing Grounded Theory*, 3rd ed. (Los Angeles, CA: Sage, 2008), 65–66. Robson, *Real World Research*, 477–478.

[144] Robson, *Real World Research*, 478–479.

[145] Peter Honey and Alan Mumford, *The Learning Styles Helper's Guide* (Maidenhead: Peter Honey, 2006); Peter Honey, *The Learning Styles Questionnaire*.

[146] Chifungo, "An Oral Hermeneutics," 51, 185.

[147] Coffield et al., *Learning Styles and Pedagogy in Post-16 Learning: A Systematic and Critical Review*; Tina Stavredes, *Effective Online Teaching: Foundations and Strategies for Student Success* (Oxford: John Wiley & Sons, 2011), 53.

[148] Anderson, "Cognitive Style and Multicultural Populations," 6–7; Stavredes, *Effective Online Teaching*, 54.

[149] Chifungo, "An Oral Hermeneutics," 123.

[150] Nhiwatiwa, *How We Preach*, 65.

[151] Sadler-Smith, Eugene, "Cognitive Style and Learning in Organisations," in Riding, R. J., and Stephen G. Rayner (eds.), *International Perspectives on Individual Differences, Volume 1: Cognitive Styles* (Stamford, CT: Ablex, 2000), 190.

[152] Howles, "African Learning-Style;" Honey, *The Learning Styles Questionnaire*; Honey and Mumford, *The Learning Styles Helper's Guide*, 2000.

[153] Howles, "African Learning-Style," 29–35.

[154] Honey, *The Learning Styles Questionnaire*, 24–25; Honey and Mumford, *The Learning Styles Helper's Guide*, 2006, 20–21.

[155] Joy and Kolb, "Are There Cultural Differences in Learning Style?"

[156] Sadler-Smith, *Cognitive Styles*, 190–191.

[157] Guild, "The Culture/Learning Style Connection," 16–21.

[158] Honey and Mumford, *The Learning Styles Helper's Guide*, 2006, 25–37.

[159] Groves, *Reading Romans at Ground Level*, 76.

[160] Anderson, *Choosing to Preach*; Beatriz Munoz-Seca and Cassia Silva Santiago, "Four Dimensions to Induce Learning: The Challenge Profile," IESE Business School, University of Navarra (2003), 5–6, 9.

[161] Munoz-Seca and Santiago, "Four Dimensions to Induce Learning: The Challenge Profile," 5.

[162] Sadler-Smith, *Cognitive Styles*, 190–191.

[163] George L. Roth and Anthony J. DiBella, *Systemic Change Management: The Five Capabilities for Improving Enterprises* (London: Palgrave Macmillan, 2015); Gilbert W. Fairholm, *Leadership and the Culture of Trust* (Westport, CT: Greenwood, 1994); Fiona Graetz et al., *Managing Organisational Change*, 3rd ed. (Milton, NSW: John Wiley & Sons Australia, 2012); David E. Hussey, *How to Manage Organisational Change* (London: Kogan Page, 2000); John P. Kotter, "Leading Change: Why Transformation Efforts

Fail," *Harvard Business Review* 85:1 (2007), 96–103; Cliff Moyce, "Culture Change," *Management Services* 59:1 (2015), 28–30; Martin Orridge, *Change Leadership: Developing a Change-Adept Organization* (Farnham: Gower Publishing, 2012); Edgar H. Schein, *Organizational Culture and Leadership* (Oxford: John Wiley & Sons, 2010); Harsh Pathak, *Organisational Change* (New Delhi: Pearson, 2010).

[164] John Stott, *The Contemporary Christian* (Leicester: Inter-Varsity Press, 1992), 24–29.

[165] David K. Strong and Cynthia A. Strong, "The Globalizing Hermeneutic of the Jerusalem Council," in Craig Ott and Harold Netland (eds.) *Globalizing Theology: Belief and Practice in an Era of World Christianity* (Grand Rapids: Baker Academic, 2006), 139.

[166] Strong and Strong, "The Globalizing Hermeneutic of the Jerusalem Council," 127.

[167] Ramesh Richard, *Scripture Sculpture: A Do-It-Yourself Manual for Biblical Preaching* (Grand Rapids: Revell, 1995). Chifungo, "An Oral Hermeneutics."

[168] Myles MacBean, "The Homiletic Window: A Model for Reflective Preaching Praxis," *Evangelical Review of Theology*, 41:3 (2017), 209–221.

[169] Bowers, "Theological Education in Africa: Why Does It Matter?" 149.

[170] H. Grady Davis, *Design for Preaching* (Philadelphia: Fortress, 1958), 11.

[171] BUILD Partners <http://buildpartners.org>

[172] Ramesh Richard, *Scripture Sculpture*.

[173] BUILD Curriculum, <http://www.buildcurriculum.org>

[174] Chifungo, "An Oral Hermeneutics," 130–181.

[175] Patterson, *Ministry by the People*, 52; Holland, *Ministry by the People*, 109; Kinsler, *Ministry by the People*, 1983, 1.

[176] Kinsler (ed.), *Ministry by the People*.

www.ingramcontent.com/pod-product-compliance
Lightning Source LLC
Chambersburg PA
CBHW071510150426
43191CB00009B/1468